PARK
Mountain of Treasure
CITY

by

LARRY WARREN

MOUNTAIN PRESS PUBLISHING COMPANY
MISSOULA, MONTANA
2004

Park City: Mountain of Treasure

Text © 2003 Larry Warren

First Printing, 2003
Mountain Sports Press

Second Printing, 2005
Mountain Press Publishing Company

Library of Congress Cataloging-in-Publication Data

Warren, Larry, 1950–
    Park City : mountain of treasure / by Larry Warren.
        p. cm.
    Includes bibliographical references and index.
    ISBN 0-87842-507-1 (cloth : alk. paper)
    1. Ski resorts—Utah—Park City—Management. 2. Ski resorts—
    Utah—Park City—History. 3. Park City (Utah)—History. I. Title.
        GV854.5.U8W37 2004
        979.2′14—dc22

                                2004025619

Printed in Hong Kong by Mantec Production Company

Mountain Press Publishing Company
1301 South Third Street West
Missoula, MT 59801
406-728-1900

TO MATTHEW, MEGAN AND ANDREW
You may leave Park City,
but Park City will never leave you.

Contents

FOREWORD

By Bill Marolt

President/CEO, U.S. Ski and Snowboard Association

It's been many decades since the U.S. Ski Team was invited to Park City to develop a year-round training center for our athletes. As I think back to the old mine buildings on top of what is now Park City Mountain Resort, and our old offices on Main Street, I'm reminded of how far Park City has come as a resort community, and how far we have come as a team of athletes striving to be best in the world.

Fall is a great time of year in Park City. I gaze out my office window at the bright golden aspens amidst a sea of evergreens lining the slopes of Park City Mountain Resort. Slowly but surely, as the first snows arrive, you can watch the line of white descend from the peaks above Jupiter Bowl to the steep face of C.B.'s Run and the gladed descent down Payday. It's a sign that another winter season is just around the corner—a time that re-energizes skiers and snowboarders.

Park City has always been a community of vision and dreams. It dates back more than a century when the silver mines blossomed and Park City was thriving. In the latter half of the 20th century, the silver turned to white and the vision of Park

20th century, the silver turned to white and the vision of Park City turned to snow. Today, Park City Mountain Resort is a premier destination for skiers and snowborders.

Our dream and vision for the U.S. Ski Team had its roots right here in Park City. In the summer of 1974, the Team made its home here. Three decades later, Park City remains the home of the U.S. Ski and Snowboard Team.

People often ask why the U.S. Ski Team is based in Park City. Frankly, our athletes travel the world all winter. But many of them make their permanent home right here in Park City for the very same reasons that recreational skiers and snowboarders from around the world gravitate here: the quick drive from an international airport, the consistency of the "Greatest Snow on Earth," the diversity of lifestyles and activities, and, most of all, the people of our community who have followed their dreams and vision, and made Park City a unique winter playground!

It was the vision of Edgar Stern who first brought the Team to Park City. But it was the dreams of Nick Badami and his late son Craig who put the real spark into the mountain. Nick and Craig had the vision of what it took to become a major resort. And we're proud that much of that early vision was built on the worldwide visibility of our U.S. Ski Team athletes and now our snowboard team, too.

Winter means not just recreational skiing but competitive ski racing and snowboarding in what's become a win-win situation for both sides, Park City Mountain Resort has parlayed its World Cup races and the Chevy Truck U.S. Snowboarding Grand Prix events into international calling cards for the resort. Believe me, Europeans know all about our town and Park City Mountain Resort.

Nick Badami is, without question, one of the best businessmen I have ever met. And Craig was a marketing genius. Together, they laid the groundwork to develop what became one of the world's finest resorts. Now, under the leadership of an equally talented young businessman, John Cumming, Park City Mountain Resort—with its Olympic legacy—is known worldwide.

Park City got its chance to become a World Cup stop almost by accident in March 1985 after races had been weathered out in Europe. Craig Badami jumped at the opportunity. That was a historic moment (though we didn't realize it at the time). Nick and Craig, two of the most to-the-bone, committed Ski Team supporters, gave us a chance for more World Cups in the U.S. The other little-remembered fact is how Park City Mountain Resort showed the Europeans how vital snowmaking is, especially for early season skiing.

Over the years, America's Opening has single-handedly changed the face of World Cup ski racing, and it has set the tone for what Park City Mountain Resort has become as an international destination resort.

As I travel with our athletes to resorts around the world, I'm always drawn back to our home in Park City. I think what sets this resort apart from so many others is that it's a community, which has retained its history. You see that in the old mine structures around Park City, and in the tasteful architecture at the base village. And you sense it in the locals who also make the mountain their home, welcoming visitors from around the world.

I grew up in a ski community, and it's what I love. This is a true ski community. People live here to ski. You can cut school or take a lunch break from work and be on the lifts in five minutes.

I'm proud to call Park City my home, and the home of the U.S. Ski and Snowboard Team. I was especially proud in 2002 when six of our record 10 ski and snowboard Olympic medals were won right here at Park City Mountain Resort. It was the complete accomplishment of the vision and dreams set forth by Park City's forefathers many decades ago when they set out to build a world-class mountain resort. ⚒

❀ INTRODUCTION ❀

You know the feeling: It's day three or four of your ski vacation, and you start fantasizing about moving permanently to the mountains. Those thoughts fade once you return home, or you manage to repress them, but during your next ski vacation they come back as strong as ever.

At some resorts, you know it would never work. The place is beautiful but too isolated or too small or too fake for any kind of real life. Living the ski life there would require two jobs or starting a backbreaking seasonal business. A real career, like the one your parents thought you'd have after college, seems almost out of the question in a setting like that.

That's what makes Park City so special. Four decades ago, when the struggling old mining town turned to skiing as its salvation, it had an ace in the hole for both visitors and those who wanted to live the ski life: There was already a ribbon of asphalt up Parley's Canyon from Salt Lake City and its international airport—a drive of 45 minutes or less to Park City.

There were other attractions as well. The first skiers who came, and the generations who followed, couldn't help but be charmed by historic Main Street and the houses stacked on the slopes above. Even today, the town's real and faux Victorian architecture takes you back to the dawn of the previous century. And the ski mountain looks friendly, its gnarly peaks and bowls hidden from view. The combination of town and the mountain results in what *SKI* magazine readers have consistently rated as one of the top 10 winter resorts in North America.

When you add in Park City's accessibility, you have the last piece of the package. In Park City, a resident can live in a major ski resort and work in a metro area of nearly a million people, with all the amenities that that entails. For the past 20 years I have lived the ski life while pursuing a television news career that is available only in a city. And I've honed the drive to work to a mere 32 minutes. (Don't tell the Utah Highway Patrol.)

When I originally came here, Park City was much smaller and less known. The only gated communities were communities of cows. Back then, there were genuine Park City characters still around who'd lived their lives in a mining-turned-ski town. Will Sullivan, a retired miner who was mayor in the early 1960s, held

court in the cafe of the old Alpha Beta store. He told me of the times he had felt duty bound to endorse his mayoral paycheck back to the city to help pay the municipal bills. Art Durante ran Art's Hardware on Main Street, before upper Main was high-priced real estate. Art never went to the trouble of updating the prices marked on any lingering inventory, and savvy shoppers knew if they rooted around in the back of a dusty shelf long enough they'd find a 15-cent widget exactly like the 50-cent one displayed in front, all the time enduring Art's good-natured insults.

I feel privileged to have known those who lived here before the resort era and who hung on during hard times when others gave up and moved away. Their stories of town life before skiing are both funny and touching. In the 1920s and '30s, Thon Gin grew up in Chinatown, which happened to be in Swede Alley just east of Main. He lived with his parents and 11 siblings in a two-room uninsulated shack—the front room devoted to the family laundry business. In the 1920s, '30s and '40s, Bob Birkbeck, the foreman of the Judge Mine shop, organized ski outings that started with a trek through the mine tunnels and a ride up the hoist to Thaynes Canyon, where he and his guests put on skis that they had waxed with melted wax cylinder recordings for extra glide.

Other native Parkites tell of growing up as either "upper-enders" or a "lower-enders," depending on which end of town they lived in. The distinction was geographic rather than economic—both ends were equally poor. With no outside reference point, the children of that era thought the whole world lived as they did, and they took joy in their surroundings, never thinking of themselves as economically disadvantaged. The creeks, ponds and mountain meadows were their summer playgrounds, and the winter brought sledding and ski jumping. When Otto Carpenter and Bob Burns hand-built the pioneering Snow Park lifts, they started downhill skiing, never imagining where it would lead.

Like many, I planned to live the ski life here for just a few years and then move on, but I soon found myself hooked. Park City is a place where you can find real people, fantastic skiing and a close metropolitan area full of opportunity. My two years have stretched past two decades now, and there is no end in sight.

—Larry Warren

PARLEY'S PARK

Rich Martinez calls himself "the Ol' Miner." It says so on his well-worn burgundy and mud-colored wide-brim hard hat. The license plates on one of his cars reads OL MINER. The plates on another reads 9 KIDS. Martinez and his wife, Leona, have been busy during a lifetime in Park City.

Martinez looks like a tough old working man. Now in his 70s, he is proud to talk about his 50 years underground and to show a visitor a small portion of the labyrinth of tunnels where he toiled. On this day we board a mine cage and drop 1,500 feet below the surface to the bottom of the Number 3 shaft of the legendary Ontario Mine. There, Martinez points out the sights. "Some of the old timbers in here are over a hundred years old," he says. I check them for cracks—and hope they'll hold up at least for another hour.

"Come over here, I'll show you something," he says, as we walk along a wet, sloppy tunnel. We're heading toward the vein of ore Martinez first mined in 1950. The only light comes from our battery-powered headlamps, but I'm not especially worried, because I've got Martinez with me. And if everything goes to

LEFT: FIRST KNOWN PHOTOGRAPH OF PARK CITY, TAKEN BETWEEN 1882 AND 1884, LOOKING NORTH TOWARD THE SNYDERVILLE BASIN. ABOVE: MINERS OF THAT ERA USED HAND DRILLS AND HAMMERS TO DRILL BLASTING HOLES, THEIR WORK ILLUMINATED ONLY BY A CANDLE.

ABOVE: EARLY PROSPECT HOLES WERE DUG BY HAND.
MOST MEN ABANDONED THEIR CLAIMS IN THE
WINTER. RIGHT: A FEW WINTERED OVER, USING SKIS
OR SNOWSHOES FOR TRANSPORTATION.

hell, I've got my "self-rescuer," a small device I'm supposed to breathe through if we hit carbon monoxide or other deadly gases.

"I'm going to light a candle to see if we've got any oxygen back there," Martinez explains, striking a match that briefly illuminates the entire stope, or excavation. The candle burns steadily, so we continue walking. Martinez picks up a discarded piece of iron and starts scraping away at a foot-wide rock formation that looks different from the rest of the rock in the tunnel. A few scrapes and a vein of ore sparkles in the light of our headlamps.

"See that stuff right there? See that? That's the stuff we're looking for. That's lead...zinc. It'll have silver and gold mixed in with it."

I stare at the small slice of precious metals just like some wide-eyed prospector in Park City's early days. Then Martinez points to his candle, which is burning ever lower. "We gotta get out of here," he says, blowing out the candle. We retreat to the main tunnel with better ventilation, and then to the hoist where we climb into the cage and ascend back to the surface and fresh mountain air.

Veins of ore like the one Martinez pointed out were the reason Park City became a town in the first place. The story begins back in the Cretaceous Period, perhaps 140 million years ago. The earth's many layers were still forming and moving. Molten magma from the earth's core was pushing outward, bulging the

sediments higher and higher, building mountains.

Earthquakes shook the ever-tilting sediments, sending shock waves through them like lightning bolts, opening faults and cracks. About 30 million years ago—a heartbeat in geologic time—molten liquids called hydrothermal fluids bubbled up and flowed into the faults and cracks, like caulk squeezed into cracks around a windowsill, filling the voids. The fluids cooled, and the minerals in them clung to the host rock around them and

NOMADIC UTE INDIANS WERE THE FIRST HUMANS TO SPEND TIME IN THE PARK CITY AREA.
ARCHAEOLOGISTS HAVE DISCOVERED THEIR FIRE RINGS IN THE SNYDERVILLE BASIN.

crystallized. These ore veins would remain hidden for millions of years until a future civilization considered them precious enough to dig for them.

As you drive west into the Wasatch Mountains from Salt Lake City, you can see how this process worked, and how the mountains were formed, by looking at the folded sediments standing nearly vertical in every canyon. Behind you, opposite the western slope of the Wasatch (commonly referred to as the Wasatch Front), lies Salt Lake Valley, 4,400 feet above sea level, the economic, cultural and population center of Utah. As you continue driving east, you'll cross the crest of the Wasatch at 7,028-foot Parley's Summit and descend the eastern slope of the Wasatch (sometimes called the Wasatch Back). The valley here lies 2,000 feet higher than the one abutting the Wasatch Front, and at the south end of it lies present-day Park City.

Early natives passed through this high basin. The winters were too long and snowy for year-round settlement, but the Utes made summer camp here for generations, hunting and gathering the bounty of the high mountain valley. Archaeologists have found their fire pits in the area.

According to Ute legend, the Creator, Senawahv, put sticks in a bag to create people. A troublesome coyote ripped the bag open, scattering the people everywhere. Senawahv looked into the bag and found a few sticks left. "This small tribe will be Ute. They will be very brave and able to defeat the rest," he declared. For centuries the Utes ruled over Utah and Colorado.

The Utes had the land on both sides of the Wasatch to themselves until 1847, when a band of religious refugees drove the first of many wagon trains over a trail blazed a year earlier by the California-bound Donner Party. The Mormons, led by Brigham Young, were seeking a place far enough away from American civilization to find peace and a spot to create their ordered society. Unpopular beliefs like polygamy and charismatic leaders like founder Joseph Smith and his successor, Brigham Young, had attracted scorn, hatred and violence in the Mormons' previous homes in New York, Ohio, Missouri and Illinois.

Once they reached the Salt Lake Valley, the Mormon pioneers struggled, and even faced starvation, but persevered and eventually flourished. Right from the start Brigham Young sent Mormon colonists throughout the empty lands between the Utah Territory and southern California—people like church apostle Parley Pratt.

RIGHT: MORMON LEADER BRIGHAM YOUNG, IN THE SILVER DISCOVERY YEAR OF 1868, URGED HIS FOLLOWERS TO IGNORE MINING RICHES IN FAVOR OF BUILDING AN AGRICULTURAL SOCIETY IN UTAH (ABOVE).

Pratt decided to try to make a living in the mountain basin he'd first spotted in 1847 while scouting ahead of the original Mormon wagon train. He ran cattle on the belly-deep grasslands of the basin, and he built a toll road down into the Salt Lake basin through a gap in the mountains still known as "Parley's Canyon." In 1850, he collected $1,500 in tolls from gold seekers heading to California, a handsome return on investment in those days. Over the years, his wagon road evolved into a section of the Overland Stage route, the first transcontinental road, the Lincoln Highway, then a state road, and finally Interstate 80.

As time went on other Mormon settlers moved into the high mountain basin east of the Wasatch. Heber C. Kimball established a stage stop there. Samuel Snyder traded a yoke of oxen for some basin lands near a forested slope and started a sawmill, which came to be called Snyderville. Today when you exit I-80 at the junction named for Kimball, the flat land you see all around you is the area known as the Snyderville Basin.

Throughout the early years of Mormon settlement, Brigham Young ruled as both territorial governor and Mormon president and prophet. In 1857, a U.S. justice assigned to Utah Territory wrote to President James Buchanan, complaining that he had little or no authority among the Mormons. Buchanan responded by sending the U.S. Army. Mormons feared attack and prepared for the "Utah War." No shots were ever fired, and the soldiers camped harmlessly 35 miles southwest of Salt Lake City—until they were ordered back East at the start of the Civil War.

Utah was now the key to east-west movement across the nation. The Pony Express, the transcontinental telegraph, the Overland Stage and soon the first transcontinental railroad would all pass through the Mormon stronghold. The new president, Abraham Lincoln, sent army units back to Utah to protect this essential east-west corridor and to keep Brigham Young from siding with the Confederacy.

Instead of sending regular units, the Army recruited a colonel turned California gold prospector and mining entrepreneur named Patrick Edward Connor to raise volunteers (most of them gold prospectors) from California to return to Utah. Connor set up a camp (later called Fort Douglas) on the benchlands above the Mormon capitol, and, according to legend, aimed a cannon at Beehive House, where Brigham Young lived with his 27 wives and 53 children.

The two sides maintained an uneasy peace. Then Connor came up with an unorthodox strategy to fight an unorthodox opponent. What Utah needed, he reasoned, was a gold rush like the one he'd

seen in 1849 in California. "My policy in this territory," he wrote, "has been to invite hither a large Gentile and loyal population, sufficient by peaceful means and through the ballot box to overwhelm Mormons by sheer force of numbers." He described Brigham Young and fellow Mormons as "disloyal and traitorous to the core." Young had already preached against gold seekers. "Instead of hunting gold, we ought to pray the Lord to hide it up," he thundered from the pulpit. "Gold is not wealth! Go and raise wheat, barley, oats."

All Connor's vision lacked was the gold to start the gold rush, so he made it the duty of his soldiers to find it. In 1863 his men helped discover copper in Bingham Canyon on the western border of the Salt Lake Valley. (Nobody exploited it fully in those days, but

ABOVE: ORE WAGONS LOADING AT THE ONTARIO MINE. RIGHT: SMALL MINE OPERATORS GENERALLY SOLD TO BIGGER MINES WHEN DEVELOPMENT COSTS BECAME TOO GREAT.

it would later develop into the largest copper mine in the world, still producing today from an open pit so large astronauts can see it from space.) By 1864 Connor's soldiers were poking around the canyons of the Wasatch. They struck silver at the top of Little Cottonwood Canyon, and soon other miners founded the town of Alta there. One canyon over, in Big Cottonwood, prospectors found more silver and established the town of Brighton.

In 1866, with the Civil War over, tens of thousands of discharged soldiers and new immigrants headed for the untamed West. President Lincoln had once predicted "Utah may yet prove to be the treasure house of the nation," and that prediction was about to come true. Two years later, as miners based out of Snyderville prospected south along the east slope of the Wasatch, climbing as they went, soldier-prospectors attached to Fort Douglas were a few miles away, checking similar terrain. The prospectors found silver ore at 9,300 feet along a ridgeline they named Pioneer. They filed the Young America claim just before Christmas and, a month later, the Yellow Jack and Green Monster claims. The Walker and Webster and the Pinion claims would soon follow.

Meanwhile, the three soldiers, about four miles to the southeast, noticed an outcrop of yellow quartz, broke it off, and found silver ore in a vein that reached to the surface. With winter weather closing in, they dug out a sample and planted a stick with

a bandana attached to it to mark the spot. This became the Flagstaff claim. When they got their Flagstaff ore sample back to Fort Douglas, assayers calculated it at 96 ounces of silver per ton. The ore sample also contained more than 50 percent lead. The following summer, the now-discharged soldiers returned to the Flagstaff and started mining.

Connor's hoped-for gold rush became more of a silver trickle. Prospectors heard of the discoveries by word of mouth, but they were getting similar reports throughout the West, so it was hard to know whose story to believe. Many prospectors used Snyderville as a base, paying storekeeper Samuel Snyder 30 cents a pound for bacon, 50 cents a bushel for potatoes and a dollar a pound for

ORE WAGON HEADING TO THE SILVER KING MINE FROM MAIN STREET IN 1891. THE CONSTRUCTION OF THE SILVER KING TRAMWAY PUT ORE FREIGHT WAGONS OUT OF BUSINESS A DECADE LATER.

sugar—premium prices in those days. Rector Steen, a former Fort Douglas soldier who'd been in on the Salt Lake Valley copper discovery, groused that Snyder's prices for mining tools were too high. Snyder charged $2.50 for a shovel and double that for a pick. Still, Steen and other prospectors kept Snyder's sawmill busy, and Steen's investment in a $5 pick would pay off soon enough.

More claims were staked in 1869, the year the big excitement nationwide was the driving of the golden spike at Promontory Point, Utah, connecting the nation by rail. The rail connection was critical. Those early miners could find ore, but without a local rail connection and big money from Eastern investors, they could do little with what they found. The first mine to produce anything was the Flagstaff, which shipped 40 tons of lead-zinc ore in 1871. Mule trains carried the ore to the Salt Lake Valley. Heavy ore wagons hauled it across the barrens of Nevada and over the

Sierra Nevada to San Francisco. There ships took it on as ballast, sailed around Cape Horn and headed for Cornwall in southwest England, where smelters purified the ore. Nearby Wales was known for extremely hard quartz cobblestones. Carrying these cobbles as ballast, the ships returned to the United States with Cornish tin miners, known as the best in the world. From San Francisco the reverse overland journey commenced, bringing the Cornish miners and the Welsh cobbles to Utah. The cobbles were used in the area's first crushing mills, where ore was separated from waste rock.

Clearly, this was no way to get rich quick, but the miners came anyway, settling in a camp around a small lake at 8,000 feet just northeast of the Flagstaff Mine and a newer discovery, the McHenry Mine. The rough shanties made from brush and lumber from Snyder's mill became the first mining settlement of

The Folded Up Town

When George and Rhoda Snyder built the first Park City home, no one thought to ask for permission to build. In the 1870s, settlement was a free-for-all.

Then came the "Michigan Bunch," a group of businessmen who arrived in town in 1873 looking for opportunities. They found one in the ownership of the new town itself. J.W. Mason, D.C. McLaughlin and F.A. Nims realized no one in town had surveyed the town site and made application to the government to build on it. McLaughlin surveyed Park City, Nims made the formal application to the government, and Mason tried to shoo new homesteaders away until the three had title.

They shipped their initial survey back to a friend in Grand Haven, Michigan, who drew up a plat map. The plat assumed Park City lay on flat ground, when in reality, hardly anything was flat. Imagine taking the map, folding it in half, and opening it up into a V shape. Residential lots were measured off every 25 feet, enough for a miner's two- or three-room cabin. Lots sold for $10 to $100.

Those who'd settled prior to the Michigan Bunch's scheme didn't take kindly to being told their land and improvements weren't really theirs. And with the generic plat map, existing houses and business buildings might cross over three or more lots. The Michigan Bunch and the townspeople fought a bitter war in the courts, but in the end the government granted ownership to the Michigan Bunch, and existing landowners had to pay the Michigan group for what they already had.

The plat map made no sense then and still doesn't today. The numbered streets—First, Second, Third and so on—run straight up hills. Many of them are so steep they were never built on. Today, some east-west streets are too dangerous for winter use. A few are blocked off every winter when a car might skid downhill and crash into a living room. On Rossie Hill, east of Main Street, not a single platted uphill road was ever built. In place of streets on the impossibly steep hills, the town built staircases. Today, on Rossie Hill, one row of houses has no street access. Residents climb up or down stairs to horizontal wooden walkways that lead to their homes.

The plat also lists avenues with names like Anchor, Daly, Chambers, Farrell, Provo, Echo, Allison, Kamas and Coalville. None of them exist.

Even today, a complicated land transaction that requires a public notice of the survey can result in a legal description that can fill a newspaper page. And the purchase price for a 25-foot lot now lies north of $100,000.

Miners walked to their steep hillside homes using a network of staircases in place of streets.

ABOVE: RHODA SNYDER AND HER HUSBAND GEORGE GIDEON SNYDER WERE PARK CITY'S FIRST PERMANENT RESIDENTS, AND GAVE THE TOWN ITS NAME. LEFT: MINERS' CABINS WERE BUILT QUICK AND CHEAP, AND LACKED INSULATION AGAINST THE WASATCH WINTERS.

Lake Flat, where Deer Valley's Silver Lake Lodge is today.

Meanwhile, Sam Snyder's brother George was looking for opportunities. As a Mormon with five wives, he followed Brigham Young's anti-mining dictate but saw opportunity in mining the pockets of the miners. He loaded his youngest wife, Rhoda, and their two children into a wagon and set off south from Snyder's mill three miles to where the canyons coming from the top of Pioneer Ridge and Flagstaff Bowl came together in a gulch with a stream. His daughter Lillie later remembered that the teamsters had to cut down big trees to get the wagons to the gulch's base, where they built a log cabin roughly where the

Town Lift loading station is today. The two-room house was quickly expanded into a miner's boardinghouse, which became the gathering place for miners who camped below Lake Flat. Everyone called Rhoda "Aunt Rhoda," a name that stuck until her dying day. For the Fourth of July, 1872, she sewed an American flag out of a white bed sheet, a red flannel baby blanket and a blue silk handkerchief, and the miners raised it on a pine pole. Until then the area had been known as "Upper Parley's" or "Upper Kimball's," but on that Fourth of July day George Snyder declared it would be called "Parley's Park City." It didn't take long before Parley's name was ignored, and one of the great mining camps—and future ski resorts—of the American West had a name that endures to this day.

THESE ONTARIO MINERS WERE LARGELY IMMIGRANTS. THEIR DAILY RATION OF THREE CANDLES PROTRUDES FROM THEIR POCKETS.

Still, Park City could have been a mere footnote to the mining history of the West if Rector Steen hadn't taken his $5 pick and knocked off a two-inch outcrop of rock in the gulch a mile and a half north of Aunt Rhoda's boardinghouse. This was just two weeks before the Snyders' 1872 Fourth of July celebration. Later Steen would write, "We found a little knob sticking out of the ground about two inches. We had this rock assayed, and it went from 100 to 400 ounces of silver to the ton." Steen's "rock" was nearly pure silver.

Steen had three partners. Years later one of them, Herman Buden, wrote to *The Park Record* with a more colorful but less believable discovery story. He had lost his horse (his only friend) to a creditor and was ready to end it all. "But with the pistol in my hand my mood changed, and I decided to try one last time," he wrote. "I was idly swinging my pick at each rock outcrop as I went along."

Then he broke off the two-inch knob and discovered the ore vein that led to developing Park City's legendary Ontario Mine.

Two weeks after the Fourth of July, 1872, the four partners filed their claim, and soon a mining speculator came along who purchased—but never executed—an option to buy it for $30,000. Another speculator, Californian George Hearst, arrived a little later, fresh from the fabled Comstock Lode in Nevada where he and San Francisco partners had already made one fortune. When that first sale fell through, Hearst bought the Ontario for $27,000. Hearst's assay of an ore sample showed each ton of it would yield $200 in silver, lead and zinc.

Hearst and his partners had enough capital to build their own smelter, the Marsac, where Park City Hall now stands. That eliminated the long haul to England and allowed the Ontario to produce $14,000 worth of silver, zinc and lead a week, double the

ABOVE: LOWER MAIN STREET WAS A BUSTLING, NOISY INDUSTRIAL AREA, WITH TWO RAILROADS HAULING PASSENGERS AND MINERALS. LEFT: THE ONTARIO MINE, WHERE GEORGE HEARST SOLIDIFIED THE LEGENDARY HEARST FORTUNE.

output of all other Park City mines combined. By late 1872, the *Utah Mining Journal* reported, "Five men are working at the McHenry Mine, and the Ontario Mine is taking out ore and looking very good. There are about 100 men in the district."

Itinerant prospectors carried the Park City news to other mining camps. With the opening of the Ontario, Park City was the new Comstock Lode, the new Sutter's Mill. Prospectors and miners all over the West were talking about it.

With the new transcontinental railroad just 20 miles away in Echo Canyon, rail entrepreneurs raced to get the mining business of Park City. The Utah Eastern railroad pulled into town in November 1881 and was soon acquired by the Union Pacific. A rival group trying to build a railroad up Parley's Canyon spent the next nine years hacking through brush, trees and rocks before their line arrived at the base of Main Street in 1890.

"We can boast of not having an idle man in the camp," the *Salt Lake Tribune* bragged in 1875. Between 1870 and 1890, two-thirds of the

The Silver Queen

Mining profits produced 23 millionaires in Park City, every one of them a story. A few of the moguls, like George Hearst, were wealthy when they came to town and only got wealthier. Others, like John Judge, John J. Daly and Thomas Kearns, worked for years with pick and shovel before finding their fortunes.

And then there was the Silver Queen.

Susanna Bransford arrived in Park City in 1884 by way of Missouri and California. She came to visit friends, but stayed, working as a seamstress at Aschheim's Mercantile on Main Street. She was tall and quite attractive and soon fell in love with Albion Emery, the store's part-time bookkeeper and the town's postmaster. The two married three months after meeting, and then Emery quit his postmaster job to become bookkeeper at John Daly's mine.

Soon Emery and two of his friends had a chance to buy out one of Thomas Kearns' partners in the Mayflower Mine. He somehow raised $8,000 and became a significant shareholder. While some mystery remains about the deal, it appears he got the $8,000 from Ontario Mine superintendent R.C. Chambers, who wanted in on the action but as a rival mine manager couldn't be up front about it.

The Mayflower merged into the Silver King, and soon enough the Emerys were rich.

Susanna Bransford arrived in Park City a seamstress and married into a fortune. she had four husbands. outliving them all. and died nearly broke.

They spent 10 years happily married, but Emery suffered from Bright's disease, a kidney disorder. Upon his death, Chambers sued Emery's widow for half of her late husband's Silver King stock. On the witness stand, though, Chambers would not admit to being a Silver King stockholder and Susanna Bransford Emery became the sole inheritor of 150,000 shares of Silver King stock. In 1902, her stock was worth $100 million; her income from dividends alone was $50,000 a month.

In Victorian times widows typically mourned for two years before taking another husband. At the end of her mourning period, Susanna married a Chicago lumber and mining tycoon, Colonel Edwin Holmes, and the two moved into the spectacular Gardo House in Salt Lake City, an elegant mansion Brigham Young had built years earlier for his favorite wife, Amelia. There they would entertain 250 guests at a time, each one entering the house by way of a red carpet that stretched from the carriage stop at the street to the front door. Susanna added an entire wing to the house to display a growing art collection, prominently featuring a bejeweled portrait of herself.

Her clothes came from Paris, but as one newspaperman wrote, "Clothes don't grace her. She graces them." When she traveled, her wardrobe included as many as 100 gowns and all their accessories. She and the colonel traveled widely. Their honeymoon alone took two years.

The couple moved to Pasadena, California, living in their mansion, "El Roble," between adventures. After 28 years of marriage, Colonel Holmes died, leaving the Silver Queen widowed again.

She moved to New York City, into the Plaza Hotel. There, single women of the era needed "walkers," or escorts, to accompany them on social outings. One of these was Prince Nicholas "Nicki" Engalitcheff, an expatriate, impoverished Russian prince who sold insurance part-time and courted the attention of ladies like Susanna.

The deadbeat prince proposed, and Susie accepted, but it turned out Engalitcheff was still legally married to another. To avoid publicity, Susanna moved to Paris.

In Paris, at age 71, she met and married a dashing 41-year-old Serbian doctor, Radovan Delitch, whom she'd known in New York social circles. Dr. Delitch was a World War I hero and a cancer researcher who moonlighted as an international playboy. Susanna proposed marriage. New York society was stunned.

By now the Great Depression was on, but the Silver Queen still spent money lavishly on clothing, jewelry, travel, gifts and entertainment. On a 1932 trip to Salt Lake City, she met with Silver King Mine partners and fellow stockholders and learned how much her assets had plunged. Meanwhile, her marriage with Delitch was in trouble. They feuded openly. Delitch stormed off to Paris, and Susanna went to El Roble in Pasadena. Delitch soon realized that his abandoned Paris medical practice was unsalvageable and got on a ship back to America to beg Susanna for another chance. En route, despondent, he hung himself out the porthole

The Silver Queen's Salt Lake City mansion, Gardo House, purchased from Brigham Young.

of his shipboard suite and was buried at sea. After hearing the news, Susanna auctioned off El Roble.

By now Nicki Engalitcheff was divorced. The two got back together and finally married. Within months the Russian was bored and chasing women half Susanna's age. Rather than divorce, the two lived apart. Shunned by New York society, Susanna went back to Pasadena, where she lived in a hotel.

Even at that age, she created a sensation wherever she went. Jack Gallivan, the *Salt Lake Tribune* publisher who was raised by his aunt Jenny, the widow of Thomas Kearns, remembers seeing Susanna at his wedding. "She was wearing a flaming red dress. I remember it well. She was a spectacular person and cut quite a fancy figure in Salt Lake, New York and Paris throughout the years."

And he treasures the story Jenny Kearns told him just before her death. "They were sitting in Peacock Alley at the original Waldorf Astoria in New York having tea," Gallivan recalls, "and the Silver Queen takes Jenny Kearns' hand and says, 'Are you still wearing that old wedding ring of Tom Kearns?' And Jenny Kearns pulls her hand away and says, 'Whose wedding ring would I be wearing?' Whereupon Susanna Bransford Emery Holmes Delitch Engalitcheff reaches a hand down her ample bosom and pulls out this long chain and on the end of the chain are four wedding rings!"

"She was a character; she was without peer," her biographer Judy Dykman marvels. "At the age of five she crossed the [Great] Plains in a covered wagon. At 16 she survived a stagecoach holdup. By the time she was in her 50s she crossed the United States in an airplane. She went around the world four times. She met Hitler, Mussolini, Roosevelt and the Pope. She married four husbands. She outlived them all."

She also outlived her $100 million fortune. By the time she died in 1942 after taking sedatives in a cheap second-floor hotel over a garage in Norwalk, Connecticut, she was living on borrowed money. To this day no one knows whether the sedatives were meant to calm her or to kill her.

ABOVE: LOOKING NORTH TO PARK CITY IN 1891, THROUGH THE SMOKESTACKS OF THE ONTARIO MILL. RIGHT: PARK CITY'S NUMEROUS SALOONS OPERATED 24 HOURS A DAY TO ACCOMMODATE ALL MINE SHIFTS.

people arriving in Park City were between the prime working years of 15 and 40, most of them male. This was a period of tremendous immigration for the United States. Northern and Western Europeans were among the first to arrive, along with Chinese who had been imported to build the transcontinental railroad. Immigrants followed jobs requiring little skill or knowledge of the English language. The Europeans became the backbone of Park City's miners. The Chinese, distrusted by nearly everyone, were not allowed below ground, but handled the camp chores of cooking and washing.

The Cornish found the silver mines much like the Cornish tin mines and were considered the most highly skilled miners in the camp. The Scots spoke Gaelic and worked and lived together at the McHenry Mine near Lake Flat. Scandinavians worked the mines and sawmills and tended to businesses. Spaniards worked alongside Swedes and Slavs. The Irish, according to

jokes of the day, gravitated toward bartending.

Hearst's Ontario was the centerpiece of the mining district, setting the standard for wages. The Ontario ran three shifts a day. In 1880, the night boss made $4.50 per shift; rock breakers, $3; engineers, $4; carpenters, $3 to $4; and skilled blacksmiths up to $5. These were phenomenal wages for the time, reflecting the richness of the ore coming from below. Utah Territorial law

DRIPPING WATER IN THE MINES WAS A CONSTANT NUISANCE. MINERS WORE YELLOW SLICKERS
AND BATTLED THE FLOW WITH PIPELINES AND GIANT PUMPS.

ABOVE, RIGHT: THOMAS KEARNS HITCHED A RIDE
INTO TOWN AND BECAME A MILLIONAIRE AND A U.S.
SENATOR. LIKE MOST PARK CITY MOGULS, HE BUILT
HIS MANSION IN SALT LAKE CITY. RIGHT: HE
INSPECTS THE SILVER KING WITH HIS PARTNER,
DAVID KEITH, ON THE LEFT.

required single miners to live at the mines in boardinghouses, and the mines deducted a dollar a day from their paychecks for room and board. In 1872, the U.S. Census counted 100 men in Park City; eight years later there were 1,000. The miners got two holidays a year—the Fourth of July and Christmas.

One day in 1883, a bindlestiff named Thomas Kearns hopped off a train near Snyderville Basin and walked into town. Bindlestiffs were itinerant laborers who rode the rails from town to town, job to job. Soon this son of Irish Catholic immigrants landed a job at the Ontario, but he wasn't a man to settle for life underground. In his spare time, Kearns prospected on his own, following the advice of his Ontario foreman, David Keith, by looking east of the Ontario, where the experts agreed no ore existed. The land was unclaimed and called the Mayflower area.

For six years Kearns struck his pick into rocks, hand dug prospect holes and believed in the luck of the Irish. One night, as his nephew Jack Gallivan recounted the story nearly a century later, Kearns' girlfriend, Jenny, was at a dance when "Tom Kearns, still dressed in his mining gear, covered with muck and mud, came down and took her out of the arms of some gentleman she was dancing with and said, "I hit it today—now we can be married. Now we *will* be married." Kearns and his partners called their mine the Mayflower but would soon merge it with other interests and

ABOVE: THE DALY-WEST MINE AND MILL. THE DALY-WEST WAS THE SITE OF PARK CITY'S WORST MINING DISASTER. LEFT: MINERS POSING IN FRONT OF A DALY-WEST BUILDING.

Ontario west to Pioneer Ridge. John J. Daly, according to stories of the day, asked the Ontario's superintendent, R.C. Chambers, if the mine's ore veins extended west. "If it did I would have had it long ago," Chambers snapped. Daly wanted more than simple pick-and-shovel work and staked his future on the Daly-West claim he explored after his Ontario shifts. Within a few years of its discovery, the Daly-West was another mining giant, paying $100,000 in cash dividends to shareholders every month.

The Daly-West was also the scene of Park City's worst mining disaster. Just before midnight on July 15, 1902, a tremendous blast rocked the mine. The powder magazine had exploded, filling the mine with fire and poisonous gasses. As families kept vigil outside, rescuers brought out 25 bodies from the Daly-West, and another nine from the Ontario, which shared a ventilation tunnel. The Utah Legislature passed a new law forbidding the storage of explosives underground, but 34 miners and their

create the Silver King Coalition Mining Co. Keith was one of Kearns' original Mayflower investors and would reap his share of its fortunes. Eventually Keith and Kearns both moved to Salt Lake City to pursue other interests and invest their money both together and separately. One of their purchases was the *Salt Lake Tribune*, which they fashioned into an alternative voice for non-Mormon Utahns. The two men would remain friends for life.

Another Ontario miner explored the area between the

Rising From Ashes

It started around four in the morning at the American Hotel, near the top of Main Street on the left. A Chinese cook tossed kerosene into a kitchen cookstove to jump start the dying embers from the night before. The coals awakened with a roar, exploding fire onto the kitchen floor. It was June 19, 1898.

The cook ran out the front door screaming, alerting a policeman, who fired three pistol shots to sound the alarm. The shots were heard at the Marsac Mill, a block east of lower Main on the shoulder of Rossie Hill, where there

ings on Main were made of wood. The winds grew stronger. The sirens at the mines awakened miners in the boardinghouses who ran down canyon to help. The phone lines were burned, but the telegraph still worked, and Chief Berry called for help from surrounding towns. As far away as Salt Lake and Ogden, firemen loaded equipment on trains and started up.

Explosives handlers from the mines blew up buildings midway down Main, hoping to create a firebreak. Blowing embers skipped right over the gap. The men set buildings on lower Main afire, hoping they would burn

Upper Main Street homes were spared as down-canyon winds pushed the flames down Main and onto Rossie Hill, to the right, and Park Avenue, to the left.

was a siren. The siren's shriek woke Parkites to an impending disaster.

Mining towns are not meant to be permanent. Miners dig, blast, muck and move on. Canvas tents like Rector Steen's give way to log cabins like George and Rhoda Snyder's, which give way to wood-frame shacks of miners and merchants. Mining camps play out, and few residents invest in the permanence of brick.

Fire shot through the roof of the American, where a common down-canyon wind caught the embers and carried them to other structures. Soon a butcher shop, barber shop and the Judge, Ivers and Keith stables were ablaze.

Volunteer fire chief Berry, a blacksmith who had a shop with his brothers on lower Main, led the fight. His son watched from the front porch of the Berry home on Woodside Avenue, two blocks uphill from Main. "He just sat on the front porch and watched it burn," his daughter, Wilma Berry Larremore, remembers.

Being June, Park City was about as dry as it can get. All but five build-

back into the main conflagration. Nothing worked. People from buildings not yet on fire ran back inside, salvaging what they could. Hotels emptied furniture with the help of guests. The stable, which had more than a hundred horses, lost only seven. One bar rolled out a piano, and the story goes (as it usually does in mine campfire stories) that a pianist happened by and banged out the song "A Hot Time in the Old Town Tonight." Those who moved their valuables onto Main Street lost them anyway, as the firestorm consumed everything on both sides of Main and everything in between.

"The demon only laughed at the puny effort and reached out its reddened tongue further to destroy," the *Salt Lake Herald* wrote. Another switch in wind direction pushed flames up Rossie Hill, sending families there running.

By 8 A.M. the fire reached Heber Avenue, just above the Union Pacific train depot. Flames stopped there on their own, just as the Coalville fire fighters arrived. Salt Lake City and Ogden Fire Departments pulled in a few hours later, in time to see only smoldering ruins.

Pre-fire Main Street consisted of substantial stone and brick buildings. In the rush to rebuild, many of them were replaced by flimsier wooden structures, some of which survive today. Bottom: Sam Raddon quickly got his newspaper back into business from this tent.

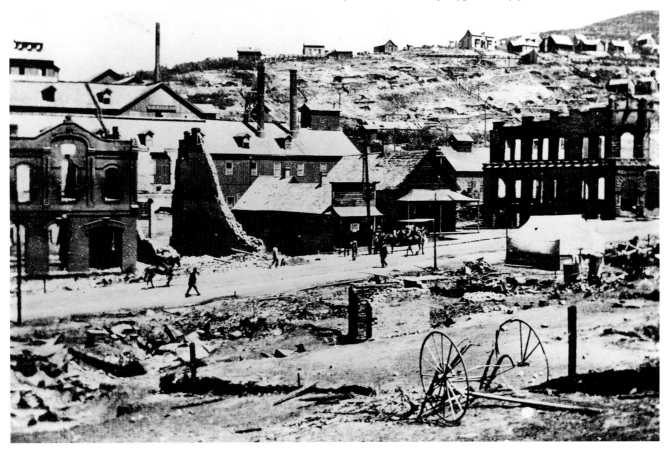

The losses were staggering. The Grand Opera House, opened just three months earlier with $30,000 in subscriptions from prosperous Parkites, was gone. Five hundred residents were left homeless. Chinatown burned completely. Two hundred buildings were gone. Damage was estimated at one million dollars. Miraculously, no one was killed or even seriously injured.

The Mormon Church's *Deseret News* wrote, perhaps wishfully, "Park City has been wiped out of existence, visited by the worst conflagration in Utah's history. It will be many years before it can be rebuilt, if recovery is at all possible."

The Park Record editor Sam Raddon wasn't going to get scooped on the destruction of his own town. Although he lost his newspaper office and all its typesetting equipment, he hustled copy down to friends at the *Salt Lake Herald*, who printed his fire edition on schedule. He quickly pitched a tent emblazoned with the words PARK CITY RECORD on its side to sell subscriptions and report on the rebuilding. "His main role was to encourage people not to give up, to rebuild," recalls his granddaughter Dixie Raddon Hethke.

Wilma Berry Larremore remembers her father's story of Park City's resilience. "People looked at the ruins and shook their heads and said, 'Park City is finished. It'll never rise from the ashes.' But there were

enough people who had the confidence, and they were completing a building a day, rushing to get it completed before winter came, and within 18 months, the town was almost completely rebuilt."

On New Year's Day, 1899, the *Salt Lake Tribune* reported: "Park City has risen Phoenix-like from its ashes."

MINERS FACED MANY HAZARDS, FROM SUDDEN EXPLOSIONS TO POISONOUS AIR TO ROCKFALLS. MINER AT LOWER LEFT HAS ONE OF HIS THREE CANDLES ATTACHED TO A "STICKING TOMMIE" CANDLE HOLDER.

families had already learned that lesson the hard way.

Life was good at the top for Kearns, Keith, Daly and Park City's 20 other mining millionaires. Their success was the dream of every hard-rock miner who stuck with the tough, dangerous work for the steady pay in the hope of finding his own silver lode one day.

Mining is a simple process. Mineralized veins lie trapped between host rock. It's a matter of breaking out the rock around the vein, lifting it to the surface, disposing of the waste rock, and sending the mineralized rock to the crushing mill, and then through the smelting and refining processes.

Miners first drilled holes in rock, initially using single- and double-jack hand drills. A single-jack drill required a miner to hold a drill bit in one hand and strike it with a four-pound hammer held in the other hand, twisting the bit to slowly break out rock chips. A double-jack needed two men, one to hold the drill and the other to swing an eight-pound hammer. Later, compressed-air drills punched the holes, creating a fine dust that destroyed the miners'

lungs and gave the drills the nickname "Widowmakers." Seldom did a pneumatic-drill operator live past the age of 50.

The only illumination early on came from each miner's daily issue of three candles. Iron spikes with a candle holder on one end held the candle. Miners called the spikes "Sticking Tommies" and jammed them in wooden supports or cracks in rock walls. The candles also served then, as now, as a warning sign when low oxygen levels posed a danger. Some Park City mines also issued miners canaries in cages for the same purpose—to take along when working in new areas where the air circulation and air quality were unknown.

Once a pattern of holes was drilled on the rock face, the miners filled the holes with blasting powder or dynamite sticks. Fuses were rigged and lit, miners retreated, yelled the warning "Fire in the hole!" and lit the fuse. Once the blast went off and the dust began to clear, muckers—a lower job classification than miners—shoveled the rock into ore cars on narrow rails. Muckers then pushed the cars down the tracks. Bigger mines used horses below ground to pull the heavy cars. The horses were blindfolded and

ABOVE: WITH COMPRESSED AIR DRILLS, DRILLING AND BLASTING WENT FASTER, BUT AT A TERRIBLE COST TO MINERS, WHO INHALED THE SILICA DUST AND SUFFERED "MINER'S CONSUMPTION." BELOW: HORSES LIVED AND WORKED UNDERGROUND INTO THE 1950s, PULLING ORE AND SUPPLY CARS.

bound up in canvas wraps to keep them calm for the trip down in the hoist. They would live below for years in blasted-out rock stables and become the miners' pets and the muckers' helpers. Cats were brought below to mouse the stables' haystacks and would take naps on the backs of resting horses. Common lore held that the horses went blind after years of darkness, but once their working days were over, they were hauled up the hoist at night and allowed to slowly readjust to the light aboveground.

The mines would last a century in Park City. Before they closed, more than 220 mining claims with silver, zinc and lead ores would be filed and mined, and $400 million in ore would be dug and blasted from the mountains. And Park City would live through the first of its two remarkable lives. ⚒

SKI RIDERS

N o one thought to record the first appearance in Park City of "skees" (or "longboard snow-shoes," as *The Park Record* sometimes called them). But they were probably introduced in the 1880s or 1890s by miners from Scandinavia. The 1900 U.S. Census counted 227 Park City residents from Sweden, Norway, Finland or Denmark.

In those days skis were used for transportation, not sport. A few early prospectors wintered over at their claims. As the snow piled up, they would work underground, stockpiling ore for shipment when the roads opened again in the spring. Mail carriers on homemade pine or hickory skis were their lifeline, delivering supplies and mail.

Early skis ran 10 to 12 feet long. Skiers carried one pole, dragging it between their legs as a brake. The binding was a leather strap passed through a hole in the sidewall of the ski and then up and over the toe of a regular work boot. To change direction, a skier would brake to a stop (or simply fall), point the skis in another direction and start off again.

LEFT: MAIN STREET IN THE BIG SNOW YEAR OF 1935. IN BIG WINTERS, SNOW HAD TO BE TRUCKED OUT OF TOWN. ABOVE: SKIER APPROACHING SCOTT'S PASS. EARLY SKIERS USED ONE POLE AND DRAGGED IT BETWEEN THEIR LEGS AS A BRAKE.

ABOVE: PARK CITY SLEDS HAD RUNNERS MADE OF OLD MINE RAIL. THEY WERE FAST AND SOMETIMES DANGEROUS. RIGHT: EMMETT "BUD" WRIGHT, AT LEFT AT THE KEYSTONE MINE. HIS SKIS ARE MISMATCHED AFTER BREAKING HIS OTHER TEN FOOTER.

Not all the early Park City skiers were Scandinavians. Emmett Ralph "Bud" Wright was born in Park City to English parents. A member of Park City High School's third graduating class, he learned the electrician's trade from a correspondence course. Park City was growing fast in the early 1900s, with telephone and power lines being strung up as quickly as technology and funds permitted. Adventurous young men like Bud Wright were perfect for jobs as telephone linemen during the winter months.

"Dad would patrol the telephone lines [on skis] between Park City and Brighton and Alta," explains Bud Wright's son, Bob. "He made his first skis himself—which was common in those days. [He] would shape the ski by hand and then steam the tips of them." Steaming the tips softened the wood. Then Wright would pass a knotted rope through a hole in the tip and hook it to a heavy weight to bend the tip and hold it in place until the wood dried permanently in that curved position.

Most people in Park City cursed the approach of the long Wasatch winter. Wagons were converted to sleighs, but uphill trips in fresh snow were exhausting or impossible, and downhill runs with a heavy load of ore, coal or lumber could be downright dangerous if a sleigh slid sideways or got going faster than the horses pulling it. Miners on long walks up canyons to the mines perished in avalanches. Cold-weather illnesses began with coughs and frequently developed into fatal pneumonia. As the winter progressed, Park City's Main Street narrowed as the piles of snow on either side grew wider. Storefronts all but disap-

peared from view behind the huge stacks of snow.

Not everybody hated winter. Town youngsters delighted in sledding down the city streets at high speed, putting fear into pedestrians. In December 1902 the city council outlawed "coasting" everywhere except Woodside Avenue. The kids flaunted the law. "Those who disregard this notice will be severely dealt with," *The Park Record* warned, but sledding through intersections continued, with the kids using a code system to warn of approaching policemen. *The Record* reported, "The police have got so far as to know [that] when a kid yells 'chisel' it means to the boys on the next corner that the police are heading that way. 'Shovel' means wait a few minutes, and 'pick' [means] all is well." As soon as police learned one set of signals, the boys changed them, and the cat-and-mouse game continued all winter.

Bud Wright and his ski buddies embraced the snow. Their enthusiasm was infectious, and within a few years, skiing as a sport started to catch on in Park City. The Park City Mountain Club formed in the 1920s, and Wright would lead as many as 50

1934
Group from Park City to
Brighton near Scotts Pass

ABOVE: A WASATCH MOUNTAIN CLUB OUTING IN 1934, HEADING FROM PARK CITY TO BRIGHTON OVER SCOTT'S PASS. LEFT: ANOTHER 1934 CLUB OUTING STOPPED AT A MINE RUIN.

one mine to another, using the mine buildings as warming huts.

Not all the skiers were locals. The Wasatch Mountain Club, founded by seven outdoor-loving Salt Lake City friends, organized trips from the west side of the Wasatch. One of the founders, Claude Stoney, had a pair of eight-foot maple skis made for him by his dad. (A Scandinavian named Peterson had shown him how to do it.) Stoney and fellow club members would catch the morning train to Ogden, change trains there and arrive at the depot on Park City's Main Street in time for breakfast at the Senate Restaurant. "We'd start off at the Senate, ski up past the Silver King Mill. We'd head over Scott's Pass and down to Brighton," he recalled 70 years later. There Stoney and his friends would dig a snow pit, line it with canvas and wool blankets and call it home for a week of ski touring. At week's end they would return to Salt Lake City by skiing out to the mouth of Big Cottonwood Canyon or over another mountain pass to the abandoned mining camp of

skiers at a time on ski outings. One route started by the Nelson farm and climbed to the King Con ridge (now served by Park City Mountain Resort's King Con high-speed quad lift). Other ski outings would head up Deer Valley to the Lake Flat area (now called Silver Lake) and back. Still other routes took skiers from

Park City Pastimes

During the 1920s, Prohibition was in full force in the rest of Utah, but you wouldn't have known it in Park City, where 18 saloons remained open, down from the peak of 27 at the turn of the century. One converted to a legal soda fountain, but 17 openly served the miner's favorite brews. Jack Gallivan, a summer resident of Park City as a youth, remembers Mike O'Connors' as a favorite saloon. "Mike 'imported'

And the proper ladies kept their distance from the line. But one day, Mel Fletcher's mother, Blanche, who was also the pianist and organist for the silent pictures at the American Theater, happened to walk past the line with a friend of hers. Park City's legendary madam, Rachel "Mother" Urban, was on her front porch and invited the ladies in for tea. After an awkward pause, the two went in. As they left, Mother Urban asked the

"The Row," Park City's red light district on Heber Avenue on the way to Deer Valley. Right, Mother Urban, madam of the row in the 1930s.

this very fine prohibition-time whiskey made of corn from Kemmerer, Wyoming, in a hearse." And, Gallivan remembers, "O'Connor featured 20 different kinds of beer, all on tap, with a sign advertising every one of them. [All] 20 beers came out of the same tap, but his patrons would go through the ritual of ordering a particular beer, and then they'd get the home brew Mike made in his basement!"

In a mining town, the third vice, after drinking and gambling, was prostitution.

In Park City, the "line" for the working girls was along Deer Valley gulch, going east from the Utah Coal and Lumber Yard. Sixteen houses were strung side by side along the north side of Heber Avenue as it headed into the gulch. Each contained a front room for entertaining, a rear room for more intimate entertaining, and a red light on the porch indicating the girls were accepting visitors. Known as "seamstresses," the girls stayed off Main Street because the madams who employed them feared they would scandalize the more proper ladies of Park City.

name of Blanche's friend. When she gave it, Mother Urban replied, "Oh yes, I know your husband well!" No record exists of the conversation that must have followed when the wife got home.

Mother Urban cut quite a figure. "Stout" doesn't begin to describe

PARK CITY BASE BALL CLUB, 1897.
WINNERS OF UTAH STATE CHAMPIONSHIP, AND PIONEER JUBILEE GAMES AT SALT LAKE CITY, JULY 20·21·22.

her girth. A parrot invariably sat on her shoulder and was said to squawk obscenities at passersby.

A Rossie Hill resident named Dick Witherow, whose front porch looked down on the line, would sit on his porch with a pad and pencil and a pair of binoculars. "And it was said of Dick Witherow," Gallivan chuckles, "that he could borrow money from any man in town!"

Life on the row had a routine of its own. There were busy nights following the twice-a-month paydays at the mines, monthly medical checkups at Dr. E.P. LeCompte's office and regular visits from officers assigned to "pull the row." At each house, the officer levied a fine of $15 on the madam for "operating a house of ill fame." Each of her working girls was fined $7.50. The fines were a regular part of the city budget and helped carry the city through lean times.

Another popular diversion was baseball. Everybody had a team. The butchers would play the barbers, and the blacksmiths would compete against the railroad men. Those who hung out at the baseball diamonds a lot, practicing, were known as BGBs (Ball Ground Bums). The mines organized their own teams for competing against those from neighboring towns and in state tournaments. Big mines like the Ontario and the Silver King could afford to hire men that were good baseball players, not good miners. Park City's mine teams were frequent state champions. (It didn't hurt that out-of-towners got winded easily when they played at 7,000 feet above sea level.) Baseball diamonds sprang up outside of town where the Albertson's grocery now stands, as well as in Deer Valley, which, with its polluting smelter and unofficial dump, was considered the poor side of town.

Two opera houses operated amid the Main Street saloons. A faro or poker game awaited in the back rooms of any number of bars. Stage plays and silent picture shows entertained Parkites at theaters like the American and the Dewey. One night during the heavy-snow winter of 1915–16, 300 people were gathered at the Dewey for a silent picture show. The rafters started creaking and groaning. The manager ordered the projectionist to speed up the movie, as the piano player raced to keep up with the action. The show ended, everyone went home, and two hours later the roof collapsed under the weight of the snow.

ABOVE: YOUNG JUMPERS ON CREOLE HILL, 1936. THE
BADGES DENOTE THE LINCOLN SCHOOL SKI CLUB.
RIGHT: JOHN SPENDLOVE JUMPS ON CREOLE, 1937.

Alta and then down Little Cottonwood Canyon. Stoney's group
pioneered classic crossings of the Wasatch and did it with
improbably primitive gear. The Wasatch Mountain Club remains
an active outdoor adventure club to this day.

With skiing becoming more popular, Park City kids began
begging their dads to make them skis. One such youngster was
Mel Fletcher, who took Bud Wright's enthusiasm and carried it
into the next generation. For his entire active life, Fletcher
would devote the winter months to skiing and teaching skiing in
Park City and the surrounding mountains. "There was a lot of
skiing here in the early 1920s," Fletcher recalls. "The kids took it
up and found they could go at a pretty good clip downhill. We
used to wrap a rope around the skis [to provide traction] so we
could walk uphill. Everyplace there was an opening in the trees
big enough, we had a little jump."

The Norwegians especially loved ski jumping. "Around

1923," Fletcher recalls, "there was a group that decided to build a jump. They built it on an old mine dump called the Creole. They cut a swath through the trees and got lumber so they could build a takeoff." On Washington's Birthday weekend in 1923, nine members of the Norwegian Young Men's Club of Salt Lake put on Park City's first ski jumping tournament on the Creole jump. *The Park Record* was impressed, saying "it will result in bringing many hundreds of people to Park City and advertising our city as a mecca for winter sports that are so attractive in other mountain cities, but none as ideal for such sports as Park City."

The Creole jump proved that ski jumping could draw big crowds of spectators who wanted to watch the "ski riders." Soon the jumpers and tournament promoters started looking for bigger and better terrain. They found it out past Kimball's Junction, along the state road heading up to Parley's Summit.

On that spot Scandinavian immigrants Christopher and Elsie Marie Rasmussen operated a roadside cafe, the Well Come Inn. Across the fields behind the cafe, Rasmussen and his three sons located a steep north-facing hill and started reshaping it into a

ABOVE: ECKER HILL IN ITS PRIME IN THE MID 1930s.
TOP RIGHT: PETE ECKER, PRESIDENT OF THE UTAH
SKI CLUB WITH ALF ENGEN (RIGHT) WHO SET
WORLD RECORDS ON THE HILL. BELOW RIGHT:
SVERRE ENGEN JUMPING ON ECKER HILL.

jumping hill with wooden takeoff ramps. The jump was called Ecker Hill, in honor of Utah Ski Club president Peter Ecker.

On New Year's Day in 1931, the Utah Ski Club sponsored its first big professional ski jumping tournament. Cars were backed up on the state road clear to Parley's Summit. A crowd in the thousands formed a half circle around the outrun and cheered with each jump and gasped at each crash. The jumpers, nearly all of them Norwegian, competed in a professional circuit with events around the country.

The crowd favorite was Alf Engen. Engen and his brother Sverre both jumped at the tournament, and both made their living on the pro jump circuit. On this particular day, Alf Engen broke the world's record, soaring 231 feet. The promoters then got on the loudspeaker and offered $500 to the man who could break Engen's new record. Alf himself took the challenge, soaring 247 feet on his second jump. "I didn't mean to jump so far," he said years later. "I thought I'd break it by just a little. That way we could keep breaking the record by a few feet each time and each make some money!"

In the summer of 1931, Sverre Engen and some other jumpers stayed over to work on the hill. They used shovels and scrapers and an old Chevy truck to hoist lumber up the steep slope. When the truck broke down, they salvaged the engine, packed the cab with dynamite and blew it to bits, just for the fun of it "We found parts of it clear down by the highway, a mile away," Sverre boasted years later. Ecker Hill would be the site of jumping tournaments until World War II.

Not everyone who liked to jump at Ecker Hill was a professional. Vern Nichol was a Salt Lake high school kid who played hooky with his lifelong friend Jack Walker so they could practice jumps on the big hill. They would "hitch a ride on a milk truck...and

ECKER HILL MEETS ATTRACTED BIG CROWDS UNTIL WORLD WAR II. ECKER IS NOW A HISTORIC
SITE AND PARK WITHIN THE PINEBROOK SUBDIVISION ACROSS FROM JEREMY RANCH.

Seeds of Decline

Park City's mining-era population peaked around the time of the Great Fire of 1898. Modern historians put the number at about 6,500. Throughout its history, Park City faced the same boom and bust cycles that would kill most of its sister mining towns around the West. There was the recession of 1893, the panic of 1907, the slowdown of World War I and more economic hardships without specific names.

ers worried, and the council passed an ordinance forbidding anyone from carrying or displaying a red flag, banner or badge in Park City. Wobblies wound up in the "dungeon" below city hall, where they used smoke from candles to write I.W.W. on the plaster walls and draw their union seal. The graffiti is still there, below what's now the Park City Museum.

In the years following the end of World War I, wages plummeted

In the 1950s, the population dwindled to 1,150, and Main Street businesses struggled. Many closed for good.

In the years leading up to World War I, mining jobs, once available to anyone with a strong back, were getting harder to secure and easier to lose. Labor unrest, rarely an issue before, took hold. In 1915, 400 Silver King miners walked out for two weeks, demanding better compensation. Two years later the surface workers at the Judge and Silver King mines, who worked nine and a half hours a day, went on strike, demanding an eight-hour day. Within a few weeks, they had it.

By 1919, the Industrial Workers of the World, known as Wobblies, were in town, organizing and agitating. They fought a mine-ordered pay cut and advocated a six-hour day, as well as the overthrow of capitalism. The threat of "Bolshevism" had the town lead-

as low as 50 cents a day as mines and miners struggled to survive. Hometown soldiers who had fought in the war now marched up Main Street, and while the men looked sharp in uniform, the stores on Main were showing signs of neglect. Within a decade, the Great Depression set in, and most of Park City's mines either cut wages to the bone, ran skeleton crews, consolidated with neighboring mines or closed altogether. Native Ella Sorensen remembers trying to keep a family fed and clothed on a miner's declining and irregular salary. She recites the verse of the times: "You use it up, you wear it out, you make it do, or you do without!"

"I was about three years old," lifelong Parkite Jim Santy recalls. "It was one of my first vivid memories. This was in 1936,

and the miners went on strike and set up picket lines. I was looking out the window—and gosh—a car came up King Road and
everybody was yelling and hollering, and they stopped it. Geez!
They tipped the thing over, drug the guy out, kicked him in the
head, got blood all over the road." Santy's memory is of the Silver
King Mine's attempt to break a strike by bringing in nonunion
"scab" miners from surrounding farming towns like Kamas,
Oakley, Coalville and Heber City. The scabs knew nothing about
the strike. They had simply been offered jobs in the mines, not
realizing the anger they were facing.

Larry Hethke, another Park City kid of the era, remembers the
same scene. "The Park City miners were waiting with their clubs,
and some of them had guns, although I don't recall a gun going
off. Everybody made their kids stay home, but I snuck down there
and kind of stayed behind the lines. It was pretty rough!"

ABOVE: EARLY ECKER HILL JUMPERS, LEFT TO RIGHT, VERN NICHOL, ROWLAND WALKER, A.L. HAMLIN AND JACK WALKER. ABOVE, RIGHT: THE LONG ARM OF THE LAW, DEPUTY SAM BILLINGS, SUMMIT COUNTY SHERIFF EPHRAIM ADAMSON, AND DODO RIDING THE HARLEY. RIGHT: JACK WALKER (LEFT) AND VERN NICHOL, STILL SKIING 70 YEARS AFTER THEIR GLORY DAYS ON ECKER.

[arrive] in time for breakfast at the Well Come Inn," says Nichol.

On one occasion, as they were jumping, "two men in hats and overcoats [came] trudging through the snow over to us," remembers Walker. "Their car, a big black sedan, said GRANITE SCHOOL DISTRICT. They'd heard about our trips to Ecker, and they were wondering why we were sluffing classes."

Nichol chimes in, "I don't think they ever reported us, 'cause they enjoyed that jumping so much."

"Yeah," says Jack, "We never did hear from the principal about that."

Events held at Ecker Hill were the first to bring awareness of skiing as a sport to Utah's masses. Tournaments were headline news in the papers. Radio station KSL broadcast them live on the 50,000-watt station heard all over the West.

Alf Engen would go on to found a number of ski areas, including his beloved Alta in 1936. He would remain there as ski school director until his death. He coached the 1948 Olympic Ski Team and was declared "Athlete of the Century" by *The Salt Lake Tribune* as the year 2000 began. His stature as one of the world's dominant ski jumpers was sealed on New Year's Day of 1931 when he set the world record twice in one day on Ecker Hill.

By the late 1930s, Utahns were deciding skiing was more fun to do than to watch other people do. They started buying skis and learning to use them at Utah's two new ski areas, Alta and Brighton, both built atop the remains of old silver mining ghost towns. The crowds declined at Ecker, and tournaments were getting more difficult to stage because the volunteers who used to help pack the landing hill were now out skiing.

LINING UP TO RIDE THE LIFT AT SNOW PARK SKI AREA, THE HAMBURGER SHACK AT RIGHT. DEER VALLEY'S SNOW PARK LODGE NOW OCCUPIES THIS LOCATION.

"I loved Ecker Hill so much, and there was sadness," Alf recalled on a return visit to the hill in the 1980s. "But it's the natural evolution of skiing. People like to ski themselves, and that was the right direction for the sport."

Meanwhile, back in Park City, President Franklin Delano Roosevelt's Works Progress Administration (WPA) was cutting ski trails. The WPA was created to get Depression-era America working. Crews went to work clearing ski runs for no reason other than to give them something to do. The organization selected the area near the Ontario Mine that locals called Deer Valley or Frog Valley as a work site.

"It was just walk-up-and-ski-down skiing," Mel Fletcher explains. Soon, ski trains chartered by the Park City Chamber of Commerce were pulling in from Salt Lake, disgorging skiers eager to try their luck on the newly cut runs.

World War II snapped the country out of the Depression, and for a short time stimulated mining for strategic minerals like lead and zinc. But gas rationing during the war killed the Ecker Hill

jumping tournaments, and most of the jumpers left to join the war effort. Many of Utah's best jumpers volunteered for duty with the fabled 10th Mountain Division. Alf Engen became a technical advisor, designing and testing equipment for mountain warfare.

After the war, local skiing buddies Otto Carpenter and Bob Burns spent weekends driving to Alta and Brighton to ski. "We said, 'Doggone it, why should we go that far away all the time when we got all these good hills in Park City?'" recalls Carpenter. The two got to thinking about the WPA runs in Deer Valley, and the pent-up demand for skiing. With a lease from the Park Consolidated Mining Co., which owned the surface rights to the Deer Valley trails, they went to work building the town's first T-bar and single chairlifts.

Carpenter, a former ski jumper at the Creole and Ecker Hill jumps and a skilled carpenter, fashioned lift towers from aspen logs piled in tepee fashion and held together with horizontal cross ties. Burns, a machinist in the Judge Mine shop, built the chair frames and wheel assemblies. Using discarded mining equipment

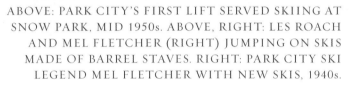

ABOVE: PARK CITY'S FIRST LIFT SERVED SKIING AT SNOW PARK, MID 1950s. ABOVE, RIGHT: LES ROACH AND MEL FLETCHER (RIGHT) JUMPING ON SKIS MADE OF BARREL STAVES. RIGHT: PARK CITY SKI LEGEND MEL FLETCHER WITH NEW SKIS, 1940s.

and all the new parts they could afford, they put up a T-bar and opened for skiers in 1946, adding a single chairlift to the top the next year, followed by a single beginner chair. Mel Fletcher and Bob Wright offered their services as ski instructors. While Burns and Carpenter kept the lifts humming, their wives served hamburgers, chili and drinks. The worst part of the job, according to Carpenter, was the daily trek up to the top of the ski run carrying a battery to start the truck engine at the top that powered a lift.

"Sometimes one battery wouldn't get it going and I'd have to go back down through waist-deep snow to get another battery and carry it back up," says Carpenter. "We had some nice crowds in here. We had people come up from the University [of Utah], we had a lot of people come from BYU, and people from as far away as Ogden came here. Our parking lots would be full every [weekend]."

Fletcher taught Park City's baby boom generation to ski at Snow Park, the name that Carpenter and Burns gave to their ski operation. "Mel was this enthusiastic young hot dog who wanted every kid in town to learn to ski," one of those boomers, Lloyd Evans, remembers.

Carpenter eventually bought out Burns's interest in Snow Park and ran it until 1969, when the last remaining mine company in town, United Park City Mines, declined to offer Carpenter a new lease. It said Carpenter could continue oper-

ating Snow Park on the land, but Carpenter said "you'd have to be a damn fool" to invest in lift equipment for ground where you could be kicked out any day.

When Deer Valley Resort opened in 1981 on the land that Otto Carpenter had walked away from in 1969, it honored Park City's ski resort pioneers by naming its base lodge Snow Park and its first two lifts, Burns and Carpenter. ⌖

Blowing Off Steam

Two miners in a saloon got to arguing in 1893 over who could drill the deepest hole in solid rock in 15 minutes. The bar talk ended in a contest on June 14th at Bonanza Flat, near the original Flagstaff discovery. Bets were placed among 150 spectators, and at the end of the allotted time, Frank Ward, with his drill turner, John Downey, had sunk their bit 17 inches, beating Charley Emery and his drill turner, Mike Sullivan.

The drilling contest became an annual town event, with prize money and plenty of side bets. It soon moved to the Fourth of July, one of the few allowed days off, and to this day it is still held, only now on Labor Day, which in Park City is called "Miner's Day." Ol' Miner Rich Martinez still presides over the mucking and drilling contest in City Park and has won it a fair number of times. In today's ski town, hardly anyone knows how to muck and drill, so many of the contestants travel from Wyoming mines for the day and a chance at putting a little prize money in their pocket for the drive home.

The Ol' Miner himself, Rich Martinez. Mucking (above) and drilling (left) during the 1989 Miner's Day Mucking and Drilling Contest.

TREASURE MOUNTAINS

P arkites were indignant in 1951 when their town was listed in the book *Ghost Towns of the West*. "There were still 1,150 of us live ghosts around then," Will Sullivan, who was the town mayor, remembered.

But if things didn't improve, ghost-town status looked like it might be on the way. Shorty Sorenson, who lived on Ontario Avenue with his wife, Ella, put in his last shift at the New Park Mine in August 1957. After that there was no work for him underground. A growing number of miners and their families faced the same bleak future.

Wilma Larremore, whose father had sat on the family porch and watched the Great Fire of 1898, sat on the same porch in the 1950s and saw a different but no less destructive scene. "Everybody was moving out. They were even moving the houses out."

Banks would not loan money on Park City homes. No one would buy them even if they had the cash. Many homeowners jacked up their houses, put flatbed trailers underneath and rolled them out of town.

COLONEL JOHN NELSON AND HIS WIFE ELIZA HOMESTEADED THE AREA
AT THE BASE OF "TREASURE HILL" IN THE 1870s. THEIR LOG BARN AND
FARMHOUSE STOOD UNTIL 1963, WHEN THEY WERE BULLDOZED TO MAKE
WAY FOR THE TREASURE MOUNTAINS BASE LODGE.

ABOVE: A 1962 PUBLICITY PHOTO SHOWING SKIING AND MINE RUINS IN THAYNES CANYON ONE YEAR BEFORE TREASURE MOUNTAINS OPENED. RIGHT: THE SILVER KING COALITION MINES LOWER TRAM TERMINAL TOWERED OVER TOWN FROM 1901 UNTIL IT BURNED IN 1982. IT BECAME THE ICON OF PARK CITY IN THE EARLY RESORT YEARS.

People in other parts of Utah considered Park City a dumpy, dying has-been and looked on the town and its residents with contempt, or at best, pity. Checks with Park City addresses were not honored in Salt Lake stores.

The only residents not fearful about their future were the children, like Lloyd Evans. "We didn't realize it was an economically depressed town," Evans says. To children of the '50s, Park City was one big playhouse. "We played in the vacant houses—nearly every other one was vacant." Many of the houses still had furniture inside. As a 10-year-old, Marianne Cone and a friend roamed the half-abandoned streets and imagined what colors they'd paint the weather-beaten miners' cabins if only they had the paint.

By now Park City's 220 mining claims had been merged into one entity, United Park City Mines (UPCM). But even this one company was struggling, partly due to decisions made in the '40s and early '50s. During World War II the military needed lead, so Park City mines produced lead and completely stopped prospecting for silver. After the war, whenever a new silver vein

was located, development costs proved too high to extract the ore. Tunnel after tunnel, shaft after shaft and building after building were closed, and as they were closed, water started flooding the underground workings.

Board meetings of UPCM were dismal affairs, each a summary of the previous quarter's losses and setbacks. Between high maintenance costs, low metals prices and union troubles, UPCM was bleeding. "It became apparent in 1957 [that] United Park City Mines had to get into some other kind of business," remembered its comptroller, LaMar Osika.

FRITCH'S GARAGE, 1948, BEFORE THE CONSTRUCTION OF SKI RUNS AND CHAIRLIFTS ON THE HILLSIDE ABOVE THAT WOULD EVENTUALLY BE NAMED "SKI TEAM RIDGE."

"Why not look at turning our surface assets into a ski area?" board member Walker Wallace asked at one board meeting. Very quietly the company began investigating the ski business. The board had seen what its own employees, Burns and Carpenter, were doing on the WPA runs in Deer Valley (on land that UPCM owned). Otto Carpenter began noticing that mine vice president and general manager Seth "Red" Droubay was spending a lot of time skiing at Snow Park, sometimes only taking a couple of runs, observing the scene and leaving.

The farsighted Wallace, whose father was UPCM president, was a real estate developer in Salt Lake City. He reasoned that since United Park owned all the mountains surrounding the town and could control—and profit from—real estate growth, there ought to be great potential for UPCM in the ski business. His own company, National Planning Research, did a feasibility study for UPCM in 1958, indicating the demand was there for

another Utah ski area. (At the time there were just two big resorts, Alta and Brighton.) There were precedents for this idea, too. Alta, Brighton and Aspen, Colorado, had all begun as silver mining towns and prospered in the ski business.

The timing was also good. National magazines were starting to do feature stories on skiing and ski fashions. Skiing was showing up in the movies. It was becoming a mainstream family activity. United Park didn't see why it shouldn't capitalize on the growing craze.

LaMar Osika went looking for investors but quickly discovered what Park City townspeople already knew—no one wanted to make loans, especially big ones, to any enterprise connected with Park City. It was discouraging. The idea was put on the shelf until the early '60s, during the Kennedy administration, when the Commerce Department started offering low-interest Area Redevelopment Administration (ARA) loans to depressed communities.

As 1962 began, United Park board member Clark Wilson was

UTAH PUBLISHERS LUNCH WITH JFK IN 1962. *SALT LAKE TRIBUNE* PUBLISHER JACK GALLIVAN, FARTHEST RIGHT, ASKED FOR APPROVAL OF THE FEDERAL LOAN THAT WOULD LAUNCH THE RESORT.

in Washington, D.C., lobbying to restrict cheap imports of lead and zinc, which were keeping metals prices down. Mine vice president Droubay asked Wilson to stop by the Commerce Department and see if they could get one of the ARA loans, since Park City was as depressed as any place in America. Wilson met with several bureaucrats, whom he described as "cold as wedges." He held out little hope for a government loan. Even so, early in 1962 United Park sent a formal application for a $1,232,000 ARA loan.

Before long, the White House called.

Jack Gallivan, a United Park board member and publisher of the Kearns family's *Salt Lake Tribune*, got a call from the White House press office asking him to assemble nine other Utah newspapermen and come to Washington for lunch with President John F. Kennedy. Gallivan and Kennedy had become friends years earlier when Gallivan gave him a tour of Salt Lake City while Kennedy was a congressman. The two had stayed in touch,

and even as President, JFK sometimes picked up the phone and asked Gallivan's opinion on Western issues. The Gallivans had also been guests at White House dinners.

On August 10, 1962, over filet of sole, JFK led a discussion of world and national affairs and closed the conversation with the question, "Is there anything I can do for you out in Utah?" Gallivan, the group's spokesman, mentioned that a little mining town down on its luck needed an ARA loan, but that the application seemed lost in the bureaucracy.

"Pierre, take care of it," JFK said to his press secretary, Pierre Salinger. Two weeks later the loan was approved.

Jim Santy grew up in Park City and returned home after serving in the Korean War. Like many before him, he married a local girl and went to work in the mines. His first job was breaking big rocks into little rocks. Then he got a job cleaning underground

CBS BROADCASTING LEGEND LOWELL THOMAS, CENTER, WAS AN EARLY BOOSTER. EARLY RESORT EMPLOYEE TIM HAYDEN (LEFT) BRIEFS HIM AS MINE OFFICIALS SETH "RED" DROUBAY AND JAMES E. HOGLE, BEHIND THOMAS, AND FIRST SKI SCHOOL DIRECTOR JIM MCCONKEY (LOWER RIGHT) LISTEN.

tunnel tracks. By this time he was already thinking, "There's got to be a better way to make a living." Then fate intervened. One day the foreman called the mine workers together and said, "We're locking it up, guys."

"That's all the notice we got," says Santy. "'Jeez,' I thought, 'this is crazy.'" Jim Santy's life as a miner was over.

He went back to school to get a teaching certificate to become a music teacher. In his spare time, to supplement his income, he took up surveying. One day early in 1963, he got a phone call. "Jim, would you like to be on a survey crew?" asked a United Park engineer. "We're putting in a gondola."

"I said, 'Where are you going to get all the water?'" Santy was thinking gondolas as in Venice, Italy, imagining mandolins and stripe-shirted gondoliers.

"He says, 'No, no, no. We're going to put it on the hill.' I said, 'You're going to put a gondola on the hill?' And he says, 'No, this is a ski gondola.' Later he showed us a picture of a gondola in the air. Until then [I] didn't have the faintest idea what he was talking about."

UPCM split into two divisions: mining and recreation. The recreation division was incorporated as Park City Land and Recreational Development Co.

Until this time Park City had never been anything but a mining town. The thought of outsiders coming in to ski, have a meal and maybe stay overnight was completely foreign to Parkites. At a community meeting after plans were under way, Red Droubay urged the audience, "If you can hang on, your property will be worth a lot of money someday." Despite these brave words, skepticism ran high.

Meanwhile, at tax auctions on the county courthouse steps in

The Sin Raid

In 1955, Park City's economy was so bad the town seemed on its deathbed. Forces outside the community, prejudiced against the town's traditional tolerance for drinking, gambling and prostitution, saw a chance to finish it off. Since pioneer times, Summit County had evolved into two socially separate communities. On the west side of the county was Park City and its evil ways. The east side—basically everything east of U.S. Highway 40—consisted of pleasant mountain valleys settled by Mormon

From outside the Oak, they watched the raid unfold.

The raiders "struck with the speed of vigilantes," the *Deseret News* reported the next day. "They didn't use lights or sirens," Kimball recalled, "but there were a lot of flashbulbs going off from photographers they'd hired to shoot the evidence."

They raided Mike's Cafe, where owner Mike Spanos sold liquor over the counter, operated blackjack tables and housed "girls" upstairs. (In

Park City police winked at illegal gambling in the saloons, but a joint county and state raid put an end to the fun in 1955.

farmers. The area was as conservative as any in Utah and held the political power, including the county seat in Coalville.

On the night of April 16, 1955, Summit County Attorney Morgan Lewis Jr. presided over what became known as the Sin Raid. An army of 60, including Utah highway patrolmen and east county farmers deputized for the night, raided three Main Street establishments simultaneously. The county sheriff was notified of the raid just 10 minutes before it went down.

Gary Kimball, one of Park City's premier historians and writers, was just walking into the Park Tavern with five friends when Park City policeman Bob Evans arrived and barred their way. "Not tonight, boys. Out!" So Kimball and friends went to an establishment down the street called the Oak. "That place was okay," he says. "They didn't break the law…much."

those days, the only legal drinking in Utah was at "bottle clubs," state-licensed establishments where members could keep liquor in their own lockers at the club. The clubs could sell only mixers or setups.) Officers led two girls out of Mike's Cafe in handcuffs, while Kimball and his friends were on the street hooting, "There goes Park City's tourist trade!"

They raided the Park Tavern, where Mike Sofinades also sold drinks over the bar and kept a big crap table and a couple of blackjack tables in the rear. According to Kimball, the Park Tavern was where high school boys could get a quart of Coors in a brown paper bag. "[Sofinades] was Greek and his English was poor, but he sure could cuss." Whenever Kimball had asked for beer, Sofinades would say, "Jesus o' Christ, what you want? Son o' bitch. You want beer? Okay, son o' bitch, last time. No more." The city

had fined Sofinades $25 every time he took the covers off his tables, so he had to have enough gamblers to recoup the fine and then some.

The raiders also hit Davitch's Bar and Grill. Joe Davitch had dropped out of mortician's school to take over the bar when his father died. Subsequently he had been appointed to the city council to fill a vacancy. He would tell Kimball and other customers, "Hell, I'm the only barkeeper in the camp who has been schooled in the art of pickling, and I can pickle my customers with a finesse the other barkeeps can only envy." In addition to selling beer to minors and serving liquor over the bar, Davitch also kept a blackjack game going when customer traffic permitted. When the raiders hit Davitch's, blackjack dealer Charley Thompson simply stepped away from the table, blended in with the customers and got kicked out with them.

The east county raiders also hit other places where prostitutes plied their trade. Nobody was home at Bessie Wheeler's—everyone assumed she'd been tipped off.

Kimball still remembers the smug, self-righteous grin on one of the deputies as he padlocked Mike's Cafe. He also remembers that Park City mayor Tom Costas was so angry he went to every padlocked establishment and told the owners they could reopen and he'd protect them with 200 deputized miners. Kimball would later write, "We saw the officers as an unlawful mob using extra-legal means to loot Park City of its heritage."

Mike Spanos was charged with keeping a house of ill repute, gambling and selling liquor illegally. But no one was gambling that night, and owning poker chips and cards was not against the law. The raiders found only a little liquor, and since Spanos was running a hotel upstairs, what was wrong with renting rooms to some single girls?

At the Park Tavern, Mike Sofinades got off lightly as well. The deputies could find only a partial bottle of liquor Mike said was for his personal use. If they'd looked closer they might have found 33 pints of liquor behind the hinged cigarette display case.

Spanos and Sofinades, both aging Greek immigrants, never reopened their businesses. Only Joe Davitch spent any time in prison. Some speculated that, because he was a town councilman and a community leader, the judge was looking to make him an example. After six months in jail, Davitch moved to Salt Lake City to become a mortician, pickling his new clients permanently.

Park City's days as a town *in* Utah but not *of* Utah were over—at least for a while.

ABOVE: "MISS BONANZA" LEADS THE BONANZA DAYS PARADE TO THE GROUNDBREAKING FOR TREASURE MOUNTAINS RESORT. ABOVE, RIGHT: PARK CITY MAYOR WILL SULLIVAN CUTS THE RIBBON TO OPEN THE COMPLETED RESORT IN DECEMBER, 1963. RIGHT: FIRST LADY LADY BIRD JOHNSON ARRIVED IN THE SUMMER OF 1964 FOR THE DEDICATION.

Coalville, the mine company bought distressed property in Park City for back taxes. But the company wasn't totally heartless. If the owner of a home showed up to bid on his own property, the mine company's buyer didn't bid against him.

May 11, 1963, was celebrated as "Bonanza Day," the official kickoff of construction of Treasure Mountains Resort. It started with a parade down Main Street with its junk-filled empty lots and boarded-up and abandoned buildings. The Park City High School band, led by Jim Santy, marched along behind a float carrying "Miss Bonanza." At the site of the gondola base terminal, where the old Nelson farm once stood, the Conoco service station operator, Tom St. Jeor, dressed up like a prospector, led two burros carrying silver ore. He dumped the ore on the ground, and a large group of dignitaries, including Utah's governor, both U.S. senators, Park City's mayor, Will Sullivan, and various councilmen and business leaders took turns whacking at the ore with picks. Up on Crescent Ridge, out-of-work miners shot off dynamite blasts in salute. It was a cold, blustery day and through the festivities, snow flurries swirled.

The United Park board of directors never expected skiing would be their sole business. They hoped only that revenue from recreation would subsidize their mining business in the slow years until metals prices improved. Skiing was to be a complementary business—but one that obviously required a whole different set of skills from those possessed by mining men.

LADY BIRD RODE TO THE CEREMONIES AT THE SUMMIT HOUSE BY GONDOLA,
ACCOMPANIED BY UTAH SENATOR FRANK MOSS ON THE RIGHT.

ABOVE: LOOKING DOWN TO THE GONDOLA ANGLE STATION, WHERE THE GONDOLA SWITCHED ITS DIRECTION. THE SPRAWLING SILVER KING MINE LIES BELOW. RIGHT: THE JUDGE MINE SHOP, WHERE MANY OF THE GONDOLA AND J-BAR PARTS WERE BUILT.

Nevertheless, miners were reassigned to the recreation division, working alongside contractors from Salt Lake City. They erected the gondola base building containing ticket sales, a ski shop, a cafeteria and rest rooms. They also built the Summit House on Pioneer Ridge at 9,300 feet, a nine-hole golf course—the major component of their "four-season-resort" concept—a J-bar beginner lift, the Prospector chairlift (where the Silverlode six-pack lift is today), the gondola and a rope tow.

The gondola was the centerpiece. It made a statement about Treasure Mountains being a serious resort, with the latest in lift technology. It would also look cool in print ads and help with marketing. The company wanted the gondola to stretch from bottom to top, 2,300 vertical feet and 12,880 linear feet. The problem was it had to clear Crescent Ridge in order to reach the summit. To do so in a straight line would put the gondola cars hundreds of feet high above Treasure Hollow and leave them dangerously exposed to wind and impossible to access in a rescue situation. So the engineers built the gondola in two stages, with the unique Angle Station near the top of the Payday run in

between. One electric motor powered the cars on the cable between the base and the Angle Station, where a second electric motor and cable loop powered the cars to the summit. An operator had to drag each loaded car through the Angle Station to make sure it attached to the second cable for the final trip to the summit. The often wild rocking that accompanied this activity gave some first-time passengers the impression that their ride was about to end abruptly.

In the old Judge Mine shop, Bob Birkbeck supervised 56 men

THE GONDOLA BASE STATION. THE RESTAURANT WAS ON THE LEFT, WITH GONDOLA BOARDING ON THE RIGHT. THE GONDOLA WAS RETIRED AND THE BUILDING TORN DOWN IN 1997.

who were building parts for the lifts. Birkbeck was another pioneering Park City skier. In the 1930s, he had led weekend ski outings, utilizing mining machinery as lifts. The trips began with rides down mine elevators, connecting to mine cars that traveled to other shafts where the skiers would ride up other elevators. They would emerge near the top of Jupiter Peak or in the Lake Flat area of Deer Valley (which the resort now calls Silver Lake). From there the group would either descend into town or head toward the little farming town of Midway, where there were hydrothermal pools to soak in while awaiting a ride home in a friend's car.

Birkbeck had some knowledge of ski lift construction because he had helped Bob Burns build parts for the Snow Park lifts in the Judge Mine shop in the '50s (after hours, of course). Now Birkbeck's group built the J-bar and hundreds of parts for the gondola. The gondola itself came from Germany, along with a German engineer to supervise the installation. The man spoke very little English. "He'd come over to the shop and draw a picture. Maybe he wants a couple of steel plates with holes in certain places, says Birkbeck. "Between broken English, gestures and drawings, we could usually make what he wanted."

Treasure Mountains topography presented marketing challenges. From the base it didn't look like a major ski mountain in the Rockies. As you look up today, Crescent Ridge (since renamed Ski Team Ridge) blocks the view of the bulk of Park City's terrain. Pioneer Ridge above that blocks much of what's beyond in Jupiter Bowl, where there are the kinds of jagged outcrops, peaks and cliffs that you'd expect in the Rockies.

Given the terrain, the early designers opted for a ridge-and-gully layout. Lifts generally followed ridgelines, and trails down the sides of the ridges dropped skiers into gullies, which led back to lifts.

Starting with the groundbreaking and continuing for the next seven months, construction ran practically nonstop. The Nelson barn and homesite became the gondola base station, with a cafeteria, ski shop and upstairs watering hole called the Rusty Nail. At the summit, an upper gondola terminal stood near the Summit House Restaurant. Run clearing, lift construc-

The Skier's Subway

Miners knew how to get up mountains. At quitting time they walked or rode mine cars back to the hoist, pulled the signal buzzer, and the hoist operator above put the gears in motion. Soon the miners were back on the surface.

From the 1920s through the 1940s, Bob Birkbeck, LaMar Osika and dozens of other mine executives used the tunnels and hoists to guide private ski parties through the Treasure Mountains terrain. They'd

rumble off. At the Thaynes shaft, they would leave Spiro Tunnel and climb aboard the Thaynes hoist, which lifted them 1,800 feet straight up to the surface.

"It was dark and wet and you'd wobble around on the tracks, and you couldn't wait for it to end," Carol Bates remembers. "But it was pretty interesting." Clark Parkinson, Park City Mountain Resort's only original remaining employee (he started before the resort opened),

Miners operated modified mining trains to haul skiing passengers underground. Skiers boarded cramped train cars for a three-mile ride under Treasure Mountains.

arrive at the Ontario or Daly West Mine hoist, ride down to catch a train, and take off underground to other parts of the interconnected mines, where other hoists would lift them higher on the mountains.

In the mid-'60s, United Park City Mine Co. used these interconnected hoists and underground trains to create the world's most unique ski lift. It was called the "Skier's Subway." Machinists built new, more comfortable cars, including a car to trail along behind carrying the skis. Old timey looking wagons carried skiers from the gondola base to the entrance of the three-mile-long Spiro drain tunnel, where they walked through an old miner's change house. (They could look up and see the suspended baskets which had once held miners' street clothes while they were underground). Then they'd climb aboard the skier's train and

remembers it less fondly. "Pitch black, claustrophobic. You'd get to the hoist and water was just cascading down (the eastern side of the mining district oozed water constantly underground). The doors would open at the top and you're just instantly frozen like a popsicle." In addition, mining machinery dripped oil and grease, which often ended up on the skiers' expensive ski wear. Once outside, skiers could access the new Thaynes chairlift, which would lift them back to the Summit House.

The mine company thought the Skier's Subway would relieve pressure on the gondola, which often had 45-minute lines, and which closed down on windy days. But the mine train ride took so long that the people waiting in line and then riding the 22-minute gondola

At ride's end, skiers gathered their skis and boarded the Thaynes hoist, which lifted them 1,750 feet, exiting the hoist building in upper Thaynes Canyon.

arrived on top first, and they'd be dry, warm, clean and inspired by the views.

In summer, the mine company ran the Skier's Subway for tourists, and one of Clark Parkinson's early duties was to supervise the summer ride program. Parkinson remembers one time when the train broke down deep in the tunnel and passengers had to walk back out. (The tunnel is so straight you can see daylight at the portal from miles inside.) Somehow a father and his son veered off the path and got lost down a side tunnel. They got out safely, but the dad let mine management know he wasn't happy.

The mine train closed for good in February, 1969. Today you can see an original Skier's Subway car in the Park City Museum on Main Street. The Thaynes hoist stands next to the bottom of the Thaynes chairlift.

ABOVE: A FEDERAL AREA REDEVELOPMENT LOAN ALLOWED CONSTRUCTION OF THE GONDOLA AND GONDOLA BUILDING IN THE SUMMER OF 1963. FIRST GENERAL MANAGER DICK STREET SUPERVISED THE CUTTING OF TREASURE MOUNTAINS ORIGINAL RUNS.

tion and new employee training all ran simultaneously.

On the winter solstice, December 21, 1963, Treasure Mountains Resort opened. The night before, workers were still installing gondola cars, and cleanup crews were still at work. The smell of fresh paint greeted everyone. But the more obvious concern for United Park's president, John Wallace, as well as vice president and general manager Red Droubay and other mine executives, was the lack of snow. At the base, grass stuck up through the thin cover.

"We had early snow and then we didn't get anymore," resort veteran Clark Parkinson recalls. "The real skiing didn't begin until January that year." Over 500 journalists, travel agents and VIP's were on hand for speeches, followed by gondola rides to the summit. There at Summit House yodelers and guitar pickers entertained. After the ride back down, the preview audience ate and drank at a reception at the lower gondola building. Everyone was thrilled with the gondola ride. The nearly two-and-a-half-

mile-long 22-minute ride had no equal in North America.

United Park was conscious of its obligation to provide as much employment as possible to townspeople. It shifted miners into nearly every position. They became lift operators, greeting skiers with everything from a cheery "Good morning" to a gruff "Get up here" or "Move it!" The miners turned lifties wore their mining clothes to the job. Instead of being helped onto a chair by someone wearing a clean uniform jacket, a skier would more likely see a miner in dirty overalls, maybe topped off with the

ABOVE: EARLY ON, THE PROSPECTOR LIFT BECAME A FAVORITE FOR ITS LONG INTERMEDIATE AND BEGINNER RUNS. LEFT: MEL FLETCHER'S MOTHER BLANCHE POSED FOR EARLY PRINT ADVERTISING FOR TREASURE MOUNTAINS RESORT, DISPENSING TONGUE-IN-CHEEK SKI ADVICE. BLANCHE SKI RUN IS NAMED FOR HER.

tors' union, but it lacked the clout to bargain itself into better pay and working conditions.

Jim McConkey, a skier with a growing reputation, was recruited from Alta to run the ski school. "He was as flamboyant a skier as Utah has ever seen," Clark Parkinson recalls. "He'd go to the highest point and ski it straight down—schuss! He had no fear, he didn't turn, he generated so much enthusiasm!" Parkinson worked for McConkey in the ski school that first year and noticed that even there, locals seemed to receive a hiring preference. "The ski school—I swear—had people who'd never been on skis." Although Parkinson was a fair enough skier at the time, he can still hear, four decades later, McConkey's voice booming down from the Prospector chairlift, "Park-in-son, bend your knees!" McConkey, a Canadian, would stay just that opening season and then return home, where he became a driving force in the development of Whistler in British Columbia.

Once snow came in abundance, the reviews were favorable. An early SKIING Magazine piece described the gondola and its Angle Station as "one of the mechanical wonders of skiing." It described the skiing itself as "some of the most interesting inter-

yellow slickers worn underground as protection against dripping water. Other miners did lift maintenance and worked on the small fleet of snowcats. The miners' wives served up food in the two restaurants and sold lift tickets. Given their backgrounds in organized labor, the lift attendants early on formed a lift opera-

The First Gondola

When United Park City Mine Co. erected its German-made Pohlig Machine Works gondola for skiers in 1963, everyone was impressed. *The Park Record* was exuberant about the new lift, to say the least. "One realizes they are not in a plane, nor a 'flying machine' of any sort, and are tempted to feel their shoulder blades to see if wings have sprouted while they are still here on Mother Earth," the newspaper said.

The truth is that Parkites had seen similar aerial lift technology for generations. Before 1901, when the Silver King tramway was built, ore from the Silver King Mine had to be hauled down Woodside Gulch in horse-drawn wagons to the rail yards at the bottom of Main Street. The trips were expensive and dangerous. When a draught horse lost its footing on an ice-covered road, the heavy wagon would often careen out of control, with sometimes disastrous consequences.

Silver King engineers went to work on the problem. Eighty buckets were attached to a 7,399-foot cable supported by 39 steel towers. The tramway ran from the Silver King Mine (near the present Bonanza six-pack chairlift) to the rail yards at the bottom of Main Street. It cost $25,000.

The tramway was powered by gravity. Buckets heavy with silver ore rode the cable downhill, while lighter loads of coal, mine supplies and the occasional hitchhiking miner went uphill.

The Silver King Coalition building at the bottom had open sides on the first floor with two sets of railroad tracks going through. Ore was dumped from the tramway buckets into two hoppers, which could load two railroad cars at a time. It took just one operator to run the whole loading operation. Completion of the tramway lowered the cost of ore hauling from $1.50 a ton to 22 cents a ton. The Silver King tramway

The first Park City aerial lift hauled ore from the Silver King Mine downhill to be loaded on trains. The towering terminal building became the resort's logo.

ran whenever the Silver King Mine was producing, carrying its last loads in the 1950s.

The Coalition building, which at 84 feet high dominated the Park City skyline, became the town's icon, the most obvious landmark of the city's mining glory days. In the early 1970s, the Greater Park City Co., second owner of the ski resort, used an illustration of the Coalition building as part of its logo. The name of the resort was in a fancy Victorian script like that used on old-fashioned mining company stationery and stock certificates.

Investors bought the Coalition building in the '60s. Supported by 12-by-12-inch timbers, it was still as solid as the day it was built. In the early '70s, the Greater Park City Co. toyed with the idea of building a chairlift to Main Street, using the Coalition building as the bottom terminal.

While awaiting a decision from the resort, the owners surrounded the building with chain link fencing to prevent vandalism, but the old structure proved too tempting a target. After a Beach Boys concert at ParkWest Ski Resort (now The Canyons), three Salt Lake City men, having missed their ride, walked back to town, hopped the fence and camped inside. They lit a fire on the floor of the all-wood structure, and the fire got out of control. By morning, the famous building was a smoldering pile of rubble. Parkites drove and walked by in steady procession, as if attending a funeral. In its next issue, *The Park Record* ran a headline that said simply, "It's Gone."

ORIGINAL SKI SCHOOL DIRECTOR JIM MCCONKEY
LEADS A CLASS DURING THE OPENING 1963–64
SEASON. HE WAS KNOWN AS A PIONEER EXTREME
SKIER AND THE NAMESAKE OF MCCONKEY'S BOWL.

mediate going in the country" that "gives every skier, at any stage of development, delusions of grandeur."

Intermediate was an apt description for Treasure Mountains Resort. It did not possess black-diamond terrain the first year, and many Salt Lake skiers scoffed at the place. "It was a wimpy place," Parkinson doesn't mind saying. "My contemporaries from Alta and Brighton would come over once and say, "Why do you ski here? Why do you teach here?" The answer he'd give them was that "it was friendly as hell. I could go up to Main Street after work to the old bars and the new bars and party and have fun." Even then the town made the difference. Park City was a real town, with real people.

"Park City became popular in a very short time, but only with locals," *Salt Lake Tribune* writer Bob Woody recalls. "It was essentially undiscovered by the outside [world]." A Vermonter who moved west to ski at Alta, Woody worked as Jack

Gallivan's business editor at the *Tribune*.

United Park wanted to do more to promote its new resort, but there were not enough accommodations in town to make it a viable choice for destination skiers. The only operating hotel that first year was the Star on Main Street. Treasure Mountains couldn't develop into a major ski resort without destination

TREASURE MOUNTAINS RESORT IN ITS INFANCY, WITH JUST THE GONDOLA BUILDING AT THE BASE. THE GONDOLA RISES ABOVE IT WITH A BEGINNER'S J-BAR ON THE RIGHT.

skiers, but the resort couldn't attract destination skiers without first-class accommodations. United Park didn't build any hotels. It spent its money on lifts and base buildings. Very little was left to mount an advertising campaign. At the end of that first season, the recreation division reported a $232,093 loss. Now UPCM was losing money aboveground (in the ski business) and belowground (in the mines).

"It was a tremendous effort to take the old town that was on its butt [and transform it into] a nice little ski town," longtime resort president and general manager Phil Jones would tell interviewers years later. Jones, a hard-working ski instructor who grew

up in the ski business, joined the recreation division in the resort's second season. "They didn't have the expertise, [and] I don't think that they had the heart to make much more of it than they did."

As the '70s began, United Park had had enough of the ski business. What the resort needed was a development company to build the tourist infrastructure to support the lift operation. The company began shopping Treasure Mountains around. Their timing was good. This was just when America's love affair with skiing was in full bloom. Over in Aspen, where another silver town was transitioning into a ski resort, an entrepreneur took notice.

A new era for Park City was about to begin. ⟍

CHAPTER 4

GREATER PARK CITY

Edgar Stern well remembers his first trip to Park City in 1968. "I was a little shocked at how everything was terribly run down, particularly Main Street," he says. It had been a century since Colonel Connor's soldiers found the silver that set the town on its path, and along Main Street, it looked like little maintenance had been done since then.

Stern came to Park City at the urging of a friend and partner in California real estate development, Warren King. King and Stern were both avid skiers and smart businessmen who were convinced American ski resorts were not keeping up with growing demand. Stern had already been successful in ski-town real estate, developing Starwood, a community of luxury homes near Aspen. He and King were looking for a promising ski area to develop. When King heard that United Park City Mines was looking for a buyer for Treasure Mountains, he called Stern and said, "You must come to Park City."

Stern had grown up in New Orleans, grandson of the chairman of Sears, Roebuck & Company. After service as a radar maintenance officer in World War II, he put his technical skill to work in the fledgling

LEFT: PARK CITY AT THE BEGINNING OF THE GREATER PARK ERA. THE MINER'S HOSPITAL IS BEHIND THE GONDOLA BUILDING. IT WAS LATER MOVED TO CITY PARK. ABOVE: THE INTERSECTION OF THE PAYDAY CHAIRLIFT AND THE GONDOLA.

TREASURE MOUNTAINS BEFORE THE LIFT EXPANSION OF THE GREATER PARK CITY YEARS, MARKED IN RED.

television business in New Orleans, building and running a television station. His father built an elegant grand hotel, the Royal Orleans, in an effort to recapture some of the old elegance of the city. Stern became fascinated by the hotel business, developing a second luxury hotel in New Orleans, the Royal Sonesta, and eventually turning an old Nob Hill apartment building into San Francisco's elegant Stanford Court Hotel.

With interests in skiing and hotels, Stern saw possibilities in Park City where United Park City Mines saw only red ink. "When I learned that all of these mountains were private land, I had to perk up and take notice, because in Aspen they used to moan and groan about the fact that all the land, the mountain land, was owned by the government, and you could scarcely do anything without permission from bureaucrats."

During the drive up from the airport in Salt Lake City, he learned that two-lane U.S. 40 up Parley's Canyon was going to be turned into four-lane Interstate 80. Before long Park City would be a short freeway hop from an international airport. "Nothing

else like it existed in the country," Stern recalls. "That's the whole beginning of it."

As for Treasure Mountains itself, Stern was not impressed. "It was not professionally done. It didn't have the right exposures. [The skiing experience] was terribly slow. You'd ski a few minutes, and [then] you were back at another lift." The mine company didn't try to gloss over the deficiencies. "They admitted it was not professionally done, and that this was not their thing. They were looking for someone to come in and redo the whole thing."

Stern and King had a mutual skiing friend in Aspen, Stein Eriksen. As Eriksen remembers it, "I bought property from Edgar in Starwood when I lived in Aspen, and we had become friends. [It was] 1969, I was [at] Snowmass, and my contract there was over. I'd been to Alta before, and I knew Alf Engen there, and I knew what the mountains were like, so I went over in the fall of 1969 and said, 'Edgar, if you can get it, take it—and bring me with you.'" That's how Stein Eriksen, Olympic gold and silver medalist and at the time the single most recognizable skier on the planet,

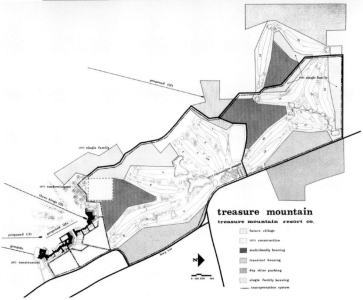

treasure mountain
treasure mountain resort co.

☐ future village
☐ 1971 construction
■ multi-family housing
▨ transient housing
▨ day skier parking
☐ single family housing
···· transportation system

N↑

0 100 200 400

ABOVE: EDGAR STERN ARRIVED FROM ASPEN WITH A VISION TO TURN TREASURE MOUNTAINS INTO AN ALL INCLUSIVE RESORT DEVELOPMENT, COMPLETE WITH CONDOMINIUMS AND RESIDENTIAL SUBDIVISIONS. LEFT: THE 1971 CONCEPTUAL PLAN.

left glamorous Aspen to become the public face of a tiny ski resort few outside of Utah had ever heard about.

Negotiations with United Park City Mines took some time, and at first Stern's group managed the area for the mine company while working on their expansion plans. They changed the name from Treasure Mountains to Park City Resort. It both tied the town and resort together with one name and reflected Stern's future plans to make Park City a "resort" experience. The logo was written in Victorian script, very much like the writing on a stock certificate from one of the mines. The Silver King ore loading station, the town's most dominant landmark, became the icon of the renamed resort. On February 16, 1971, *Salt Lake Tribune* business editor Bob Woody covered a press conference announcing the changing of the guard. "The new owners of Park City Resort outlined a program they say will involve an investment of more than $100 million in the area in the next 10 years," he wrote in his column the next day. The new company operated under the name Greater Park City Corp.

Stern's group was well capitalized. The investors included large pension funds and the Union Bank of California. They had

ABOVE: STEIN ERIKSEN FOLLOWED EDGAR STERN FROM ASPEN TO PARK CITY. ABOVE, RIGHT: GENERAL MANAGER WOODY ANDERSON GOT STERN'S MASTER PLAN UNDERWAY AND THEN LEFT FOR HIS OWN AREA IN IDAHO. RIGHT: PHIL JONES BEGAN HIS PARK CITY CAREER AS A SKI INSTRUCTOR.

a much bigger vision of Park City and the ski business than United Park City Mines ever imagined. Park City would now become a destination ski area where guests would find modern condominium lodging, an expanded lift and trail system with 20 new lifts (at build-out), an 18-hole championship golf course, trap and skeet shooting facilities, tennis courts, swimming pools, a health spa, horseback riding and hiking trails, camping and boating facilities, and new subdivisions of private homes, all part of a multiyear master plan costing more than $100 million. The plan was breathtaking, especially for longtime Parkites.

"It was difficult to make [local] people believe that one day this was going to be a great area," Stern says of those days. "They'd sit and listen, but they really wouldn't get into it." But the ski area and the town were being transformed.

"It didn't take very long to start," Phil Jones recalls. "They seemed to have so much money, and they were spending it fast." The tall, handsome and elegant skier arrived at the resort in its second year, 1964, as a ski instructor. "The Three Kings Condominiums [from studios to four bedrooms, starting at $15,000] were all sold before they were out of the ground," he remembers. Jones was an Idaho native who grew up in the ski business at his father's Magic Mountain area near Twin Falls. He'd worked for Woody Anderson

EDGAR STERN'S ALL-STAR TEAM IN 1972, AS DEVELOPMENT AND EXPANSION PLANS WERE TAKING OFF.

at Anderson's Brighton ski shop, The Wood House. From there he spent a year teaching at California's Snow Valley. When he came back to work for Woody again, it was at Treasure Mountains.

The youthful, low-key Anderson had recently been named general manager by the mine's new president, longtime mining engineer Jim Ivers. When Greater Park City took over operations, it moved Jones into Anderson's ski school position. Both men, used to the slow pace of Utah's mom-and-pop day area ski business, were in for a wild ride.

The way Stern and King envisioned it, the big money would be in real estate sales but the hook would be the skiing. For the 1971–72 season, Greater Park City Corp. spent $7 million on the mountain alone. In a trade magazine ad showcasing its new management team, the company trumpeted the fact that the "Top Team in the Ski World is now at Park City." Stein Eriksen was

director of skiing. Phil Jones, the 1971 "Ski Instructor of the Year," was ski school director. Woody Anderson, a charter member of the Professional Ski Instructors of America (PSIA) and cofounder of its Intermountain Division, was general manager. And Friedl Pfeifer, a champion skier, director of the Aspen Ski School, creator of Buttermilk ski area and pioneer ski area designer, was listed as the director of planning. They set out immediately to triple uphill capacity and expand the trail system in one construction season. First, they built the original Payday lift, a double chair serving a marquee run previously accessible only by a rope tow from the gondola Angle Station. They built the Crescent lift below the Angle Station to what was then called Crescent Ridge (now known as Ski Team Ridge). They added a second double chair, Lost Prospector, to handle the expected traffic on the other side of Crescent Ridge. Best of all, the Payday–Crescent–Lost Prospector lift combination gave the resort a desperately needed

ABOVE: ARTIST'S CONCEPTION OF GONDOLA PLAZA. THE FINISHED PROJECT WAS FAIRLY CLOSE TO THIS VISION. RIGHT: THE NEW PLAZA BASE CONSTRUCTION WAS COUPLED WITH AN AGGRESSIVE EXPANSION OF LIFTS AND TERRAIN.

second route to the summit, previously reached only via the slow—and frequently wind-affected—gondola.

To add beginner terrain at the base and lift access to the new Three Kings Condominiums, Pfeifer designed the Three Kings lift and its beginner/intermediate runs. Willy Shaeffler, ski coach of the NCAA-powerhouse Denver University Pioneers and lead coach for the U.S. Ski Team, came over to help lay out new runs off Crescent Ridge. He created the mountain's first serious expert terrain, runs originally called Men's GS and Ladies' GS, and today called Willy's, in his honor, and Erika's Gold, for champion Swiss racer Erika Hess. The runs were part of the new National Training Center for the U.S. Ski Team, which Stern pledged to build.

With four new lifts and miles of new runs, Greater Park was anxious to get the word out to pull in the real estate buyers. Stein Eriksen hit the ski convention and ski club circuit nationwide.

"Stein was really good for the ski area," says Anderson. "I was with him in our booth somewhere at a ski show, and two ladies came walking up with big smiles. I could see the gears clicking,

GOVERNOR CALVIN RAMPTON CUTS THE RIBBON, OPENING THE THREE KINGS AREA, DESIGNED BY ASPEN PIONEER FREIDL PFEIFER AND BUILT BY STERN'S CONSTRUCTION CREWS.

and by the time they got to us, Stein greeted them by name. He was an absolute primo guy at that personal stuff."

"He's one of the best salesmen I've ever seen," Stern adds. "He's got quite a feel for it. He would ski with people and take them out and tell them all these wonderful things that were going to take place. We were hoping he would encourage people to get into some real estate opportunities in town, and a great many of them did."

The following season, lift and terrain expansion continued with the King Con lift near the site of the old King Consolidated Mine, on the western side of Crescent Ridge. This provided better access to powder glades and expert skiing in one

direction, and it opened wide intermediate runs that returned skiers to the King Con chair. To flatten the pitch toward the bottom of King Con, summer trail crews bulldozed in tons of cleared trees and branches and covered them with dirt. When the ski season began, employees were horrified to see that snow would not stick to this section of the run. Beneath the dirt, bacteria were decomposing the piles of tree trunks and limbs, which warmed the ground. Snow melted as soon as it hit, leaving the center of the run a morass of mud. The run was renamed Hot Spot, and the run next to it, a short mogul pitch, was called Combustion. The next summer, crews smothered Hot Spot with dirt taken from Combustion.

With a national ski boom underway, investors were eager to buy into the new Park City. After Three Kings came the Crescent Ridge condos; they were an immediate success. Then came the Payday condos, lining the golf course. Lots in two new subdivisions, Thaynes Canyon and Holiday Ranch, sold briskly, and the first new homes in Park City since the 1950s started rising—homes that were a far cry from a miner's cabin on a 25-foot lot.

The new lifts, the arrival of Stein and a well-funded advertising

Home of the U.S. Ski Team

For years, U.S. Ski Team alpine competitions director Willy Schaeffler would bend supporters' ears about the benefits of having a year-round training center for his athletes, and for those coming up in the ranks. When Edgar Stern, who headed the group that now owned Park City Resort and who had known Schaeffler in Aspen, heard him, he offered the old mine buildings at his new ski area, and the money and materials to fix them. It would be a feather in the new resort's cap to call itself home of the U.S. Ski Team's Training Center.

At the U.S. Ski Association's November 1972 board meeting, the organization agreed to the idea, and soon the *Salt Lake Tribune* reported, "The facilities will accommodate approximately 100 racers and coaches. Jumping hills of 25, 45, and 60 meters are to be constructed and slalom slopes and cross-country trails will be constructed."

Area manager Woody Anderson told the paper, "It means immediate recognition that Utah is an area with superb skiing conditions. If the USSA ski teams pick Park City for their training, it has to have a great deal to offer."

Anderson's crews set about getting things ready for scheduled use by the next year. He promised to spend $100,000 or more, and volunteers and hired crews started tearing out old walls and mining-era debris in the buildings, cutting new runs on Crescent Ridge called Men's GS and Ladies' GS, building a long new lift called Ski Team Lift for use by racers only, and acquiring a surface lift for a shorter training run that Ski Team members themselves were cutting. Crescent Ridge thereafter became known as Ski Team Ridge.

"We went to all the training centers in Europe, every one of them," Anderson recalls 30 years later, describing the research the resort did for the training center it planned to build. "But by the time we got into it, we [the Greater Park City Corp.] were into the Park Avenue condos." The unsold condos were the downfall of Edgar Stern's ownership group, and the training center idea sputtered away as the Greater Park City Corp. concentrated on survival.

The obvious fact that escaped everyone at the time was that winter

Ski coach Willy Schaeffler. His vision was to put all ski team athletes under one roof at Park City.

athletes could not train at Park City in the winter because that's when they were traveling the country and the world on the racing circuits. "We never used it," coach Harald Schoenhaar recalls 30 years later. "The team had to train in the off-season where there was snow. We went to Mount Hood, later on we went to Portillo, Chile, and then in the fall we went to the European glaciers."

Still, the U.S. Ski Team liked Park City, with its close international airport, as a permanent headquarters, and relocation of team headquarters to Park City took place in the summer of 1974. Schoenhaar, newly hired by alpine director Hank Tauber that summer, was the first employee to arrive. "I'm German. I like to drink beer," he laughs, so he crossed the street from the Claimjumper Hotel, where he was staying for five dollars a night, and asked for a beer at one of the remaining miners' bars in town, the Cozy. "The guy gave it to me cold, and I don't like cold beer. Someone found some that was warm and I drank that."

After the relocation was complete, Schoenhaar went back to the Cozy and a regular looked up at him, and then at the bartender, and said, "I'll have another round here," he said, "and a hot beer for the goddamn Kraut!" "I never forgot that," Schoenhaar says with a laugh. "I loved it!"

The first Ski Team headquarters was an old grocery store on Main that gushed water every time snow melted or it rained. Soon Nick Badami took over the resort and took the Ski Team under his wing, moving it into better resort-owned commercial space in the newer Treasure Mountains Inn on upper Main.

It was a fortunate convergence: an underfunded U.S. Ski Team moving into a ski town just as the go-getting, high-energy, ski-loving, father-son Badami team was also moving in. While Nick pitched in to help straighten out the big picture, Craig, a racer back in his Pocono days, threw himself behind the team's athletes. His philosophy held that what's learned in racing in terms of equipment and technique trickles down to the recreational skier, and those who ski recreationally ought to support the team. The team in those days sometimes sent U.S. racers to Europe with one-way

These race-quality runs were cut specifically for U.S. Ski Team training. The run on the left was Women's GS (now Willy's), and the right run was Men's GS (now Erika's Gold.)

tickets, hoping to raise money for the return leg during the racing season. Its credit was shot, and the team had to pay cash when dealing with companies that knew its condition.

"In those days you wondered how they would survive," the senior Badami says. "When we got here, USST owed the resort $445,000 and had a lift lying in crates at the bottom. They owed a lot of money to a lot of creditors, using non-existent equipment as security." Badami wiped the debt off the books, and both he and Craig threw themselves behind the now hometown team.

Craig Badami paid for summer training camps in Park City, and promised some team athletes post-racing career jobs in the ski industry so they could concentrate solely on racing. When FIS rules changed to allow athletes to accept money from sponsors, he was among the first to jump in with headgear sponsorships. He adopted the U.S. Women's Team as his cause, and soon Tamara McKinney, Diann Roffe, Eva Twardokens, Park

City local Tori Pillinger and other American women were wearing headbands that said "Park City." The athlete's became known as "Craig's girls," and soon several were standing atop World Cup podiums, spreading the Park City name further and further.

Years later, at the 2002 Olympics at Park City, Eva Twardokens would pay tribute to Craig for that early support. "Craig was such a huge supporter of us as skiers. He really made us feel like rock stars when skiing was still an obscure sport in the United States."

Today the U.S. Ski and Snowboard Team and its sister organization, the U.S. Ski Association, remain based in Park City, now funded with corporate sponsorships and foundations to a level that assures maximum athletic performance without the financial distractions.

"It's the right place. The team needs to be in the mountains; it needs to be in a ski community," Team CEO Bill Marolt says, nearly 30 years after the team's move. "It's just going to get better and better."

A PENSIVE MODEL IN A GREATER PARK CITY ADVERTISING CAMPAIGN.

GREATER PARK CITY PLAYED UP THE MINING/SKIING CONNECTION IN ITS ADVERTISING. ABOVE: WOODY ANDERSON RIDES THE MINER'S QUADRICYCLE. LEFT: THE PRESENT MEETS THE FUTURE UNDERGROUND.

and promotion campaign started bringing in out-of-state skiers. Meanwhile, the complexion of the resort workforce changed as ex-miners retired or found more suitable jobs. Many of them could now sell their cabins on the hillsides above Main Street for $4,000 to $8,000, a big paycheck for a local who had been through the tough times of the 1950s. Many of them took the money and got out for good. "A lot of people moved to Salt Lake," says artist and miner's daughter Marianne Cone. "There was resentment about this huge company coming in and making vast changes. Warren King was called King Warren by the locals."

Cone's husband and fellow artist, David Chaplin, arrived in 1963 as one of the town's first ski bums. "Recognition of the skiing came slowly, but every year there was a little more, and by the early '70s, people's heads were spinning."

Airfares from Southern California were cheap, and the drive time was only about a dozen hours. Young Californians started showing up looking for jobs to support their passion for skiing.

ABOVE: STEIN ERIKSEN'S STAR QUALITY ALWAYS DREW A CROWD. RIGHT: INSTRUCTOR PHIL JONES.

They rented homes for $50 a month or camped out in the resort parking lot, running extension cords to the resort buildings to power electric heaters for their VW buses. The Miner's Hospital, then on the corner of the resort parking lot, became the Palace Flophouse, a skier's hostel advertising "Champagne Accommodations at Beer Prices" ($6 a night). The three-story brick hospital was later moved to City Park and remodeled into the city library. On Main, if a building was in decent shape, someone opened a business in it. The most visible segment of the population were hippies and ski bums, most of them young and virtually all of them from California. To native Parkites these young people might have come from another planet. The population started to separate into two separate cultures—native and hippie.

"[The locals] didn't like the fancy ski instructors at all," says Harry Reed, who arrived in 1963 as a instructor. "Mostly guys

IN 1902, MINERS PAID FOR THE CONSTRUCTION OF MINER'S HOSPITAL THROUGH PAYROLL DEDUCTIONS. BY THE 1970s IT WAS A SKI HOSTEL CALLED THE PALACE FLOPHOUSE WITH BUNKS PRICED AT $6 A NIGHT.

came to town, and before long [they] were chasing the local girls. The local guys were not happy with us, didn't like us and threatened to beat the shit out of us!" The first of the ski bum girls didn't start arriving until the 1965–66 ski season, which leveled the playing field a bit.

The newcomers were also mostly college graduates, superimposed on a town of blue-collar miners and their families. Native Parkites were patriotic and obeyed the law (except for those disagreeable statutes about liquor, gambling and prostitution); for them conformity to the blue-collar lifestyle was ingrained. The hippies came with anti–Vietnam War views, long hair, a penchant for illegal drugs and irreverence for most everything miners held dear. Even so, some of them opened businesses—or tried to.

"One day, two hippies showed up [at] a city council meeting [to apply for a business license]," writer and then Main Street store owner Gary Kimball remembers. "One said he was Jesus Christ, and the other said he was Justin Illusion. Their application form reeked of marijuana. They didn't get their license."

"Californians became numerous," reporter and skier Bob Woody observes. "Californians knew what we had, while we did not in Utah. They brought new life, new energy, a new lifestyle. Park City became a swinging town!" The Californians also inspired the local rallying cry "Don't Californicate Park City!" a variation of a phrase popular in Colorado ski towns of the time.

Reed and Chaplin, today's elder statesmen of the ski bum/hippie culture, agree. "There were more fun bars then than there are now," says Reed, who says back then he and many like him spent an occasional night in the "dungeon," Park City's original police lockup in the basement of City Hall (now the Park City Museum). "We don't have nearly as much fun as we had in the '70s!" say Marianne Cone and

The Culture Clash of '71

If one holiday besides Christmas is held sacred in Park City, it is the Fourth of July. In 1971, the Fourth was celebrated on the fifth, since the Fourth was on a Sunday. As usual, there was a Fourth of July parade, the biggest parade of the year.

This was the height of protests against the Vietnam War, and things were tense all over the country. In addition, Greater Park City Corp. had just come to town to shake things up with big-time resort plans. Anti–Vietnam War and anti–President Nixon marches and rallies were frequent, and the hippie

One of those balloons, probably tossed playfully at a friend down on Main, missed its target and beaned the mother of a town cop as the two walked along the street at the end of the parade.

"It was the shot heard round the world," Jay Meehan would recall later. Meehan was part of the hippie ski bum crowd who were newly arrived to ride the Greater Park City wave. A policeman raced up the street in his squad car and skidded to a stop. He grabbed the balloon thrower only to have the hippie's girlfriend jump on his back.

Park City's traditional and ski-bum cultures maintained an uneasy peace through most of the 1970s expansion—except for that one day on Main Street.

movement was reaching its zenith. Young people regularly challenged their elders and refused to follow expected norms of behavior and dress. The more conservative part of the populace was seething. But no one in Park City that morning knew that tempers would boil over in a matter of hours.

On the Fourth of July it was hard to find a more patriotic bunch than the miners. Mix in the Elks, Eagles and other patriotic fraternal orders that were hanging on in town, and then sprinkle in the irreverent, fun-loving, drug-taking, authority-flaunting hippie ski bum element—and you have the makings of a culture clash.

It all started when a water balloon went astray.

"I went to the Fourth of July parade," recalls David Chaplin, who eight years earlier had been one of Park City's first ski bums. "There were the locals and the other folks with whom, I guess, I was still identified. I saw some of the hippie types on the roof of the Poison Creek drugstore and the Oak Saloon, and they were throwing water balloons."

"It [grew] from there," Meehan recalls. "There were fistfights up and down the length of Main Street." Police backup was called in, and soon all roads into and out of Park City were sealed off by the Utah Highway Patrol, the Summit County Sheriff's Office, the county's jeep patrol and anyone else happening by with a badge. Park City was locked down.

Meehan saw it all. The miners went into the bars, he says, and "anybody they thought was a hippie or a newcomer, a pinko or a drug addict, they tossed him out and worked him over big time."

For the next week Meehan thought himself a marked man. "I was living in the Miner's Hospital (then called the Palace Flophouse), and I walked around with a baseball bat. I never left home without it."

The *Salt Lake Tribune* editorialized that maybe Park City townspeople ought to loosen up while the newcomers ought to tone it down. It was the first and last major clash of its kind. A new community of old-timers and newcomers began forming—and is still evolving to this day.

David Chaplin, who insist that "'70s parties were the best!"

But Park City's blue-collar natives saw it differently. "1971?" says Ella Sorenson, whose ancestors homesteaded just outside town a century earlier. "That's when the insanity began."

Edgar Stern and his partners had a vision for Park City that embraced quality in everything they did. It was a way of doing business Stern had learned in the luxury hotel business. To assure guests of a quality experience, the company built and decorated the condominiums and had its own property management unit to rent them. It operated its own food and beverage services on the mountain and at the base. It ran ski shops and souvenir shops in the resort's commercial space. It did its own engineering and construction and hired its own real estate sales force. It had an interior decorating division. It owned the commercial space in the big Treasure Mountain Inn Condominium on Main Street. Each of Greater Park's many divisions was headed by a vice president,

ABOVE: SKIERS AT THE THAYNES HOIST BUILDING.
ABOVE, RIGHT: PIONEER PARK CITY SKIER MEL
FLETCHER RAN THE SKI PATROL DURING THE
GREATER PARK CITY YEARS.

each of whom drove a company-issued blue Chevy Blazer. The joke around town was that it seemed everyone who worked for the company was a vice president.

A 1972 review of Utah skiing in *SKIING* magazine offered this advice: "[Park City] is a good place to start a ski tour of Utah, partly because its mountain is somewhat more kindly than those of Alta and Snowbird, and partly because it's one of the most agreeable towns anywhere." Eastern ski writer John Skow's report continues: "The mountain is big, friendly, and—for the present at least—served by more lifts than accountants could justify."

The new lifts, along with all the new condominiums and base buildings and the vacation homes sprouting up in the Thaynes Canyon and Holiday Ranch subdivisions, severely taxed the power grid. Resort general manager Anderson pleaded with Utah Power and Light to upgrade its power delivery system to the town, but his pleas fell on deaf ears. During the Christmas holiday period, the power drain was so great that the lifts slowed or stopped. "Every Christmas the power would go out," Anderson says now. "We did everything we could to beat Utah Power up on that."

The go-go years of the early '70s started fading by 1974, and cracks started appearing in Greater Park's finances. In the world beyond the Wasatch Mountains, the Arab oil nations flexed their muscles for the first time with an oil embargo. Decreasing production brought rapidly increasing prices, and when oil went up,

UPPER THAYNES WITH THE COVERED CONVEYOR SYSTEM AT THE THAYNES HOIST, AND THE
CALIFORNIA-COMSTOCK MILL JUST ABOVE. OVER IT ALL, THE STEEP BOWLS OF JUPITER PEAK,
UNTOUCHED IN THE GREATER PARK CITY ERA.

DEVELOPER WARREN KING, LEFT, WITH PHIL JONES, AS THE GONDOLA PLAZA NEARS COMPLETION.

so did everything else. Inflation took hold. President Nixon tried wage and price controls, but that had little effect and was scrapped, and besides that, he was starting to get distracted by a matter called Watergate. When Nixon resigned, Gerald Ford took over and launched his "WIN" campaign to "Whip Inflation Now" with equal, ineffectual results.

The price of mortgages spiraled upward. The real estate market went the other way. In these increasingly troubled times, Greater Park City Corp. continued with its most ambitious condominium project of all, the Park Avenue Condominiums, on the east side of the golf course.

"The Three Kings project sold as it was completed," recalls Bob Wells, who was the "closer" on Greater Park City real estate projects (and who remains a vice president of Edgar Stern's Deer Valley Resort today). "Crescent condos sold [just as quickly]. The third project, Payday, didn't sell as fast, and with the Park Avenue project, interest rates went through the ceiling."

The Park Avenue project, one-, two- and three-bedroom condos, was priced at $30,000, $60,000 and $90,000. Stern's group bit the bullet and conducted what longtime Parkites now recall as "the Park City fire sale." Prices were slashed to 50 and 60 cents on the dollar. The units finally sold, but at a substantial loss. Greater Park City Corp. was teetering under a mountain of debt. Skiing was supposed to be the hook that got investors to spend big money on real estate. Instead, lift ticket sales were the only profitable part of the company.

When trying to purchase supplies and equipment, resort employees were being told they had to pay cash. "I'd go down to Rick Warner Ford in Salt Lake, and when they heard I was from the resort they'd throw me out!" Phil Jones recalls.

Woody Anderson resigned to become his own boss, purchasing the one-chairlift Pomerelle Ski Area near Burley, Idaho, a throwback to the days of mom-and-pop ski areas. "If I was going to work 24 hours a day," Anderson says, "I figured I ought to at

A 1974 PARK CITY FREESTYLE COMPETITION. BOTH PARK CITY AND PARKWEST (NOW THE CANYONS) WERE PIONEERING VENUES DURING THE 'HOT DOG' ERA.

least be working for myself." Before he left, Stern and Warren King asked him who he'd recommend to take his place. "Phil Jones," he replied without hesitation.

By the winter of 1974–75, Greater Park City Corp. was for sale, and Jones was spending time guiding potential buyers around the property. "GREATER PARK CITY TALKS WITH DIS-NEY," read the headlines of a *Salt Lake Tribune* article in February 4, 1975. "I spent a lot of time with those people," Jones remembers. "They had a lot of high-powered people there, the Disney president, the Disney daughter. They had a photographer with their group, and every time he changed film, he would throw his carton and film can on the ground. I kept thinking, 'What kind of guys are these?'" Each time Jones discreetly picked up the litter.

In the end Disney failed to reach terms with Stern's group. The company that made Mickey Mouse a star had previously been

stalled in its efforts to build a ski resort at Mineral King in California when environmental groups like the Sierra Club fought them all the way to the Supreme Court. Frustrated once again, Disney executives left town and never did get into the ski business.

After Disney, Vail Associates from Colorado arrived to start negotiations but left in the middle of a meeting without explana-tion and never returned.

During its first eight years, United Park City Mines got the ski area off the ground and kept it running, if not always smoothly or profitably. For the next five years, Edgar Stern and associates turned a largely local's ski area into a modern destination resort and opened the door to an incredibly energetic '70s ski scene that revitalized a dying town. But with both Disney and Vail Associates backing out of a deal, only one hat remained in the buyer's ring.

"Nick Badami," a board member said. "We'll have to call him." ↗

THE
BADAMI ERA

"I didn't take up skiing until I was 48, and it was all because of Craig," Nick Badami explains as he winds up telling of his days in the ski business. Nick Badami was born of Italian parents (from Sicily) in Manhattan's Little Italy and raised in New Jersey. He started his career in the rough-and-tumble New York garment business, eventually reaching chairmanship of the clothing conglomerate BVD, known famously for its underwear. He had a knack for turning around struggling companies.

The Badamis—Nick and his wife, Avis, and their son, Craig—had a weekend place in the Pocono Mountains of eastern Pennsylvania, on a golf course with a small ski hill. They kept Craig busy with dancing lessons, horseback riding and swimming. Craig's passion was football, but he was just too small for that sport. When he was 13, his parents rented him skis for a Pocono ski lesson. He threw them to the floor of the living room, saying, "I don't want to learn another thing."

The Badamis could be persuasive parents, and soon Craig was skiing, and loving it. He couldn't wait for the next weekend, and Nick and Avis wore a path to the slopes for him. Craig started ski racing in

NICK BADAMI (ABOVE) BROUGHT SKIING TO MAIN STREET.
LEFT: THE MOUNTAIN PRIOR TO THE CUTTING OF CREOLE AND QUITTIN'
TIME RUNS. THE TOWN LIFT FOLLOWED THE LINE OF THE ORIGINAL
SILVER KING TRAMWAY.

ABOVE: NICK BADAMI TOOK UP SKIING AS A FATHER-SON ACTIVITY WITH HIS ONLY SON, CRAIG. RIGHT: CRAIG, RUNNING GATES AT THE FAMILY RESORT.

Pennsylvania, New York and New Jersey. One winter the Badamis went to St. Moritz, Switzerland, for Christmas, and Nick finally gave skiing a try himself

At age 50, Nick Badami decided to retire from the garment business. He kicked around business and investment opportunities, and at the dinner table one night he asked, "What would you say if we bought a ski area?"

Craig said, "Wow." It was his senior year in high school. That fall Craig went off to attend the University of Denver. Nick and Avis retired to California, near Avis' family in the San Francisco area. Nick's friends laughed at the thought of retirement for the hard-charging business executive. They were right to laugh.

"Retirement lasted nine months and I got bored," Nick recalls. As a skier who was a businessman, he'd observed that ski resorts were run by skiers, not businessmen. What the ski business needed, he concluded, was someone perhaps less skilled at making turns but more skilled at making bottom lines. He had looked at Jackson Hole but didn't make a deal. A friend told him about Alpine Meadows, a struggling Sierra Nevada ski area with a commanding view of Lake Tahoe. The friend mentioned it was about to go broke, so Badami, a pilot, flew over it on the way to another meeting.

In 1970, Badami bought Alpine Meadows and started working on another turnaround project, this one far removed from the garment business. Alpine Meadows was a day area where the resort owned all the businesses, including the restaurants, the ski rental operation and various shops. Badami turned all those side businesses over to independent entrepreneurs. He decided he would be in the business of selling lift tickets and nothing else. By the end of his first ski season, Alpine Meadows was in the black.

"What I like about the ski business," Nick tells people, "is it's fun. Skiing is the only business I've been in where the employees

PRELIMINARY MARKUP OF THE PIONEER AREA. THE BADAMIS OPENED NEW TERRAIN IN A NUMBER OF AREAS, INCLUDING PIONEER IN THE 1984–1985 SEASON.

are there because they want to be there, and the customers don't have to come, but they do—for fun. And," he adds with a twinkle, "it's an all-cash business, and you don't have to carry inventory." It also seemed like the kind of business a father and son could do together. "I knew early on Craig wasn't going to be a suit-and-tie kind of guy."

Nick and Craig would take ski vacations together at other resorts as well. One trip brought them to Park City, where they stayed in the C'est Bon Hotel next to the resort parking lot. This was one of the new hotels built as Edgar Stern's group was luring destination skiers—like the Badamis—to Park City.

"Park City was famous then for Shirley the Stripper," Nick laughs. "She was the only stripper in Utah, and she danced at the C'est Bon." That wasn't on the list of activities for a father-son outing, but the two skied Park City a lot that vacation because heavy snows had closed Little Cottonwood Canyon, preventing them from getting up to Alta. "It was '72 or '73, and [Park City] was kinda funky, but it was fun; it was a fun place."

Back home a couple of years later, Alpine Meadows skier and friend Art Linkletter told him he ought to check out Park City because he'd heard it was in trouble too. It was 1975. Edgar Stern and Nick Badami started talking.

"Edgar had partners—it was a complex deal," says Badami. "All the so-called owners Edgar had were fighting each other, and it was very difficult to get them at a table together." The investors wanted out, but Stern wanted to retain enough land to build a separate high-end resort.

"It took from May to October of 1975 to get everybody to agree," says Badami. Over the summer many of the meetings lasted into lunchtime, but the only two restaurants there were Car 19 and the Claimjumper, which weren't open for lunch. "We used to go to the Mount Air Market and buy a loaf of bread and cold cuts and go back over to the condo to have lunch," remembers Badami. "We took over [management of the resort] in May, on a fee basis deducted from the purchase price." When a deal was finally struck in October, Stern kept

ABOVE: PARK CITY'S TERRAIN IS BLESSED WITH
TOPSOIL INSTEAD OF ROCKS, ALLOWING NEW RUNS
TO BE RESEEDED AND OPENED FOR SKIING WITH
MINIMAL SNOW COVERAGE. RIGHT: THE TOWN LIFT
BEGAN IN A PARKING LOT BEFORE THE LOWER MAIN
STREET DEVELOPMENT TOOK PLACE.

the land leased from the mining company property that
formed an east-west range of the mountains a little south and
east of Main Street. When better economic conditions permitted five years later, Stern would come back and start building
his wildly successful masterpiece, Deer Valley Resort. Stern
and Badami remain good friends to this day.

At Park City Resort, Badami began following the same
model that had worked at Alpine Meadows. (Craig had been
learning the business independently as a ski instructor in
Aspen.) All of Greater Park City Corp.'s side businesses were
liquidated—the rental shops, the restaurants, the construction
and decorating divisions. "We got out of every business but skiing," Nick remembers of those days a quarter century ago. "We
had downhill skiing, uphill transportation and a ski school. That
was our job. We gave everything else to the town to let entrepreneurs do their own thing. Made a big difference."

SUMMER CONSTRUCTION SEASONS WAS BUSY AS THE BADAMIS PUSHED SKIABLE TERRAIN WIDER AND HIGHER ON THE MOUNTAIN. LEFT: CONSTRUCTION OF THE SNOW HUT RESTAURANT AT THE BASE OF SILVERLODE.

The army of vice presidents were all dismissed. Most stayed around town and started their own businesses. Construction companies, restaurants, engineering firms and real estate outfits were all headed by former vice presidents of Greater Park City Corp. and their staffs, and many of them became quite successful on their own.

To the relief of skiers, all attention returned to the mountain. Badami stopped most advertising. He didn't want to attract new customers until he had improved the mountain. The lifts were still stopping because of power outages. The on-mountain restaurants didn't have sewer connections and sometimes were forced to close because of frozen or clogged pipes. And the lifts were not in all the places the Badamis wanted them.

For three years, all efforts went into fixing problems. Lift equipment was updated and new power lines were strung. Backup diesel power was installed to run during power failures. Sewer lines running from the Summit House and the Snow Hut Restaurant were laid. The on-mountain food service was leased to private operators. The Thaynes chair was replaced.

Formerly out-of-bounds terrain was opened, like Blue Slip Bowl just below the Summit House. The area had always been roped off because there was no trail out of the gulch and no avalanche control on the slope. The powder-filled bowl was a constant temptation, especially to ski instructors. The previous

THE ULTIMATE HIGH AT PARK CITY: JUPITER PEAK, 10,028 FEET. THE JUPITER LIFT HELPED PARK CITY SHED THE NICKNAME "EASY ACRES."

ABOVE: SCOTT'S BOWL FRESHIES. LEFT: THOSE WHO TAKE THE SHORT HIKE FROM JUPITER CHAIR REAP THE REWARDS.

general manager, Woody Anderson, had threatened employees with "blue slips" if they were caught there. (Termination notices then were printed on blue paper.) When Craig Badami saw it, he said, "That's got to be open," and soon a trail was cut out of the bottom and the patrol began lobbing explosive charges into the bowl to stabilize snow. Blue Slip is now one of Park City's premier powder havens after a storm.

Above the Summit House, another 700 feet higher and in another world, lay Jupiter Peak. Pioneering Wasatch skiers like Jim McConkey skied the peaks and bowls above the Summit House whenever they had the time to put on climbing skins and hike up. In Jupiter there are bowls, ridges and cliff faces, and the pitch ratchets up to as much as 45 degrees. Slide your skis over the edge of West Face, look down between them, and you'll see nothing but air and the runout at the bottom.

Craig promoted Jupiter as "out of this world" skiing. The name Jupiter actually came from a mining claim. This was the

MINING RELICS LIKE THE CALIFORNIA-COMSTOCK CRUSHING MILL IN THAYNES CANYON ADD TO THE AMBIANCE. DEEP POWDER HELPS TOO.

terrain that would establish Park City as a major North American ski resort, not because most people would actually ski it but simply because it was there. The addition of Jupiter also pushed the resort's vertical rise past the magic 3,000-foot barrier.

"We tried to position Park City as a world-class area," says Nick Badami. "The first thing we did was build a lift that was not necessary—called Jupiter. When we built it, the cover of SKIING magazine said, BIG-TIME SKIING COMES TO EASY ACRES. Jupiter was the first part of the repositioning of the company."

To this day, Jupiter rarely draws enough of a crowd to create a lift line, but everyone likes to say they spent the day there even if they only skied in on the access trail from the top of the Pioneer or Thaynes lift, took a look at the peaks and the lift warning signs (DO NOT SKI THIS AREA ALONE. THIS LIFT SERVES EXPERT

TERRAIN ONLY!) and then took the cat trail out. Jupiter is the Park City you see in Warren Miller films and magazine photos. Jupiter is the all-day playground of well-conditioned hardcore adrenaline junkies who like to hike above the top of the Jupiter chair to the summit of Jupiter Peak or the top of Scott's Bowl. Of course, it's all that groomed intermediate terrain below that brings skiers back time after time.

The Badami family's methods struck a chord with everyone in the community who was tired of the frenetic five years of development that preceded them. This was a company that focused only on the ski lift business. Craig, as vice president of marketing, even changed the ski area's name from Park City Ski Resort to Park City Ski Area. "That's what we are," he said, "That's all we are—a place where you ski."

PARK CITY, 1983. THE FASHIONS CHANGE. THE SNOW DOESN'T.

CRAIG BADAMI, QUICK WITH A LAUGH, AND A SKI PASS FOR MAIN STREET EMPLOYEES. RIGHT, BADAMI WITH TWO U.S. SKI TEAM STARS, TAMARA MCKINNEY (LEFT) AND EVA TWARDOKENS

Craig—C.B., to everyone—took to marketing quickly. "I can't count the number of times a pretty girl came into the office with a note from C.B. scratched on a cocktail napkin saying, 'Give Babs a season pass—C.B.,'" says Mark Menlove, one of Craig Badami's marketing assistants in those years. "He wanted the bartenders, the waiters and the waitresses to have them because that's who tourists come in contact with. They were his underground marketing force out there."

"The most important thing to Craig was whether you were a skier," adds Charlie Lansche, another marketing assistant of that era. "If you were an unemployed ski bum, he'd sit there and buy you drinks all night."

After that first winter of Badami management, the townspeople and the mountain's skiers started feeling better about the future direction of their constantly evolving community. In addition to rebuilding the Thaynes chair that first summer, the company paved the parking lot. For more than a dozen years, early- and late- season skiers had unloaded in a muddy quagmire that got everyone's day off to an aggravating start. Paved parking was a huge hit.

Some Alpine Meadows managers moved east to fill senior management positions at Park City. One, an employee recalls, insisted that pencils be used until they were stubs and that old

ABOVE: NICK BADAMI WORKING IN HIS ALPINE
MEADOWS OFFICE WITH LONG TIME ADMINISTRATIVE
ASSISTANT ELLEN PETTEROE. LEFT: PHIL JONES
WORKED HIS WAY UP FROM SKI INSTRUCTOR TO
RESORT PRESIDENT.

letters and papers be flipped over and cut up into note paper. Frayed carpet in the offices was allowed to wear an extra year—or two. The penny-pinching drove veteran employees crazy until they realized that every dollar saved in the office was a dollar that could be spent on the mountain.

Phil Jones, who had been promoted to general manager just before Stern's group sold the ski area and now served as vice president of mountain operations, thrived on the Badami way. While Nick tended to business and Craig assumed marketing functions, the Badamis relied on Jones to manage everything on the mountain. Through United Park City Mine Co. days, the Greater Park City days and now under the Badamis, Jones had been improvising to make things work on the mountain, usually on a shoestring. Before modern grooming equipment, Jones and mining men like Loran Larsen improvised contraptions for the backs of old snowcats to try to revive old snow on intermediate terrain. They took culvert pipes and mounted them into steel frameworks, so three different pipes would roll over the snow to make primitive corduroy. Jones tried grooming snow with hay rakes like those he'd seen while growing up in southern

Mid Mountain Lodge

t weighed 140 tons. That alone should have sealed its fate. But 140 tons of old wood wasn't going to stop a group of committed Park City history buffs intent on historic preservation.

The Silver King Mine boardinghouse, built in 1901 and still occupying a spot on the hillside below the gondola Angle Station, had become a nuisance by 1987. The building stood unused, decaying, and in the way of ever-bigger snow-grooming machines, which passed on the road next to it and the Bonanza ski run.

The boardinghouse was built the same year as the Silver King tramway. Obviously the mine company was doing well then, as it built a handsome building, with a miners' dining room on the first floor and mine offices above with sleeping rooms for executives who were working late or were trapped by winter storms and couldn't get back down the mine road to town.

In its heyday it boasted a white picket fence, perfect landscaping and a gleaming-white-aproned kitchen and serving staff. As the area evolved into a busy hub of the ski area, it filled a couple of other niches. When the U.S. Ski Team attempted to establish a winter training center on the mountain for its athletes in 1973, it planned to use the building for offices, training seminars and housing for athletes and coaches. That idea never took off, although renovations for the Ski Team were underway for a short time.

Next, the boardinghouse was rechristened Mid Mountain Lodge, which served as a noon lunch stop for skiers and a place for locals to down a pitcher of beer before taking the final run to the bottom. The fact that it lay below the Angle Station worked against it. To leave the lodge, skiers—sometimes inebriated or just plain tired—had to sidestep or hike uphill to reach the point where they could ski down Treasure Hollow to end the day or catch another lift.

When the ski area planned to tear it down, preservationists were called to action. Park City historian and writer David Hampshire got on the phone.

Mid Mountain Lodge in its original location at the Silver King Mine. The Bonanza chair is in this area now, and most of these buildings have been torn down.

Harry Reed was a builder who chaired the city's Historic District Commission at the time. "David came to me trying to save it. He found that to get it down the mine road into town, it would have to be cut into three pieces," says Reed. Then there was the matter of who would pay for the move, who would stick the pieces back together again and where would it go once it was down the hill.

As the resort's president, Phil Jones knew he needed another restaurant on the mountain. He even had a spot in mind near the base of the new Pioneer chairlift, which had opened a lot of new expert and intermediate terrain.

Reed went to work. He knew the resort wanted a restaurant, and he knew Park City businessman Vince Donile might be interested in running one. All he needed was Donile's commitment to pay large-building-mover Bob Wells $50,000 to cart it uphill, with no guarantees it would arrive in the Pioneer area intact.

A tire on an axle beneath the 140-ton behemoth had blown. Donile walked up to the mover, who started to change the tire. "How many spares do you have?" he asked. "One more," came the answer. Harry Reed cracked up. Donile didn't.

An hour later (and to this day people who were there still wonder how it was possible to jack up 140 tons to change a flat), the procession began again, smoothly. The first 'dozer pushed, and the move was on. The second 'dozer added some horsepower but did not fully engage, and the third and fourth in line, and the fifth and sixth in reserve, never joined the push.

It was a startling sight to see the giant structure rolling through the aspens on a sunny afternoon. Inside of an hour, the boardinghouse arrived over its new foundation.

After a painstaking restoration, Mid Mountain Lodge is the resort's busiest on-mountain restaurant, and its most elegant. Framed mining artifacts, including a certificate of Silver King stock hand signed by Silver King mogul Thomas Kearns himself, now decorate the walls above the original wainscoting.

Upstairs, where mine executives slept, are both private dining rooms and public seating. Downstairs is dominated by the kitchen and main dining area, just as the building was designed a century earlier. Outside are distinctly modern touches—a sundeck that seems nearly the size of an aircraft carrier, and a suggestion box, positioned on a pole at the top of the roof. There's also a rather stern sign upon entrance: ABSOLUTELY NO SACK LUNCHES—EVER. After an estimated million dollars in restoration and moving costs, the owner wants to make back his investment.

"Historically in Park City, it's one of the neatest things that was ever done," Reed says. Jones adds, "It was a fun project. We all won."

"We made a sweetheart deal with Vince," Jones says of the move. "We gave him a location on the Pioneer run, ran the utilities and built a roadway—a freeway-type road to get it up there."

"We estimated the weight of the building, and I figured we'd better have that much weight in bulldozers behind it," Jones says. Donile would pay for the move, but Jones had to provide the 'dozers. Jones rounded up seven of them, with one attached in the front to steer the whole thing and six behind to push it uphill 500 vertical feet over a distance of 3,000 linear feet on the new road.

The move was to take place on September 3, 1987. Reporters, TV camera crews, preservationists and a few skeptics showed up for the show. After hours of waiting for the big moment, four 'dozers lined up behind while two more waited in reserve. The old boardinghouse began to move. Seconds later an explosion startled everyone, and the procession stopped mere feet from where it started.

Idaho. To redistribute big amounts of snow he used a John Deere earthmover not built for use on snow. Through long, miserable nights, Jones or one his workers (they'd draw straws to determine who got the honor) would drive the machine with improvised lights. There was no cab, it was dark, and it was cold. "You'd be up on the mountain on that thing that's not designed for snow and you'd always get stuck or something would break, and you'd have to walk out of there," Jones recalls.

Jones had certainly paid his dues. He spent the next few years as vice president of mountain operations, proving himself to the Badamis. In 1977 they named him president and general manager, sandwiched between the chairman, Nick, and his son, Craig, vice president of marketing.

During the height of winter, snow in the Wasatch typically falls in copious, wondrous amounts. But guaranteeing natural snow at Thanksgiving had always been problematic at Park City—at least not until enough money and technology was thrown at the mountain.

IN ITS 40ᵀᴴ YEAR, THE RESORT COULD PUMP 100 MILLION GALLONS OF WATER ANNUALLY THROUGH 150 SNOWMAKING GUNS, ENOUGH TO COVER 475 ACRES THREE FEET DEEP. SOME SNOWMAKERS ARE NEW ZEALANDERS, WHO MAKE SNOW BACK HOME DURING THE PARK CITY SUMMERS.

In 1972 the mountain opened on November 18. The next year was the best Thanksgiving for natural snow ever. But the year after that, the lifts couldn't open until December 9. In 1976–77, snow hardly fell all season as the West suffered its worst drought ever recorded. In mid February, from I-80 looking south to Park City, the mountain was brown, except for a few white ribbons. That was the year Jupiter chair opened, and its terrain was about the only part of the mountain with natural snow. Snowmaking became a bigger priority than ever before. Water lines were strung from golf course ponds over city streets to get water to every snow gun the area could scare up. Temporary lines were strung up Payday run to keep that highly visible and heavily skied run covered. All resorts in the West were in the same predicament. As an active member of the National Ski Areas Association, Nick Badami talked over the problem with fellow Western ski-area operators. They noticed that snowmaking equipment that worked well in cold, humid New England failed in the higher, drier, warmer West. The Western areas set up their own company to research and develop better snowmaking equipment. The R & D work involved testing at the Cornell University's Aeronautical Laboratory. Researchers found that better snow came from colder water, so Park City and other Western areas built refrigerators to cool already cold water to 35 degrees. Electrical compressors replaced diesel-powered

PARK CITY ON THE EDGE OF GREATNESS IN THE MID 1970s. PARK MEADOWS DEVELOPMENT IN LOWER RIGHT IS JUST BEGINNING. FLAT-TOPPED MOUNT TIMPANOGOS TOWERS IN THE DISTANCE.

PARK CITY'S LIFT PASS IS GOOD FOR 12 HOURS, EXTENDING THE FUN WELL INTO THE EVENING HOURS ON AMERICA'S LONGEST NIGHT-LIT SKI RUN, PAYDAY.

units to provide air pressure through high-pressure nozzles, which would literally cut water droplets into little pieces that would fall as snow.

Once the technology was developed, summer work crews in 1979 went to the mountain and dug trenches to bury water and air lines. Eighteen thousand feet of parallel lines went in that summer. More improvements followed nearly every summer after that, and snowmaking capacity doubled again in the summer of 1983, ironically just in time for two of Utah's heaviest snow years in generations.

Snowmaking became a huge part of Park City's winter operation. "I made the decision early on that what we were in business for was skiing and we had to guarantee downhill skiing. We had to have snowmaking to get a jump on winter," Badami says, and in Park City, the plumbing system to make snow from the Summit House on down required some amazing engineering. The benefits of snow-

making surface again every spring, when the base built up by the snow guns reappears and allows skiing to the resort's base area long after the natural snow would have become too thin and soft.

In recent years, Park City has recorded opening days on October 26, November 2, November 11 (twice) and November 14. As long as temperatures are cold enough, the area can now cover plenty of acreage to satisfy skiers when nature fails to deliver.

During those early Badami years, marketing was not a priority. But eventually, with sewer lines buried, lifts equipped with adequate electrical power and diesel generators for backup, and with a state-of-the-art snowmaking system, Park City Ski Area was ready to tell the world about its virtues.

"I would say the real [turning point at] Park City was 1978–79, after we had done our housekeeping work and the lifts were running. We [had] turned a corner," Badami declares. Park City Ski Area was ready to go to the next level. ⟋

CHAPTER 6

RACING AHEAD

As vice president of marketing for Park City Ski Area, Craig Badami had a dream job, especially for someone who loved to ski as much as he did. His assignment: Tell the world about this emerging treasure in the Wasatch at a time when the ski business was growing fast.

At first he didn't even try to lure Salt Lake City locals to Park City, because Alta, Snowbird, Brighton and Solitude were closer to the metro area. Besides, Alta and Brighton had been drawing Salt Lake skiers since the 1930s. Instead, he focused his marketing efforts on skiers from Las Vegas and Southern California, who were within driving distance of Park City. Then, starting in 1979, he went after destination skiers farther east, using Utah's dominant carrier, Western Airlines, as a marketing partner and promoting Park City as far east as Chicago. As Park City became a growing ski destination, its local skier business improved as well.

Along with paid marketing efforts, Badami (known to his friends as "C.B.") continued his guerilla marketing, spreading ski passes among the locals and making friends for the resort at every opportunity. Then

THE RESORT BROUGHT WORLD CUP SKI RACING TO PARK CITY IN THE
SPRING OF 1985. CRAIG BADAMI, ABOVE, TURNED THE RACE INTO A
WEEKEND-LONG CELEBRATION.

RACING BEGAN AS SOON AS THE RESORT OPENED. THE *SALT LAKE TRIBUNE* CLASSIC ON PAYDAY WAS AMONG THE EARLIEST. THE SILVER KING TRAMWAY TOWER IN MID RUN WAS LATER REMOVED FOR SAFETY.

he turned ski-race promoter, reasoning that if high-profile ski races could take place on Park City's slopes, major newspapers would cover those races, and every story would begin with the Park City dateline. What's more, if ski writers covering those races were captivated by Park City's Main Street, they might write about that, too, and maybe the ski mountain and its expanding terrain as well.

Ski racing had been part of the Park City scene for decades. At Snow Park ski area, ski club and school races were a regular part of the weekend activities. When Treasure Mountains opened in the '60s, early managers like Dick Street and Woody Anderson worked hard to land races. The most high-profile race was the Lowell Thomas Silver Skis Classic, named for the legendary CBS broadcaster, who liked to ski and often took his radio show on the road so as to get in a day of skiing before delivering the news. The Lowell Thomas Classic was one of the top four competitive races in the United States sanctioned by the International Ski

Federation (FIS), ski racing's governing body. The races were held midway up the mountain, above the Angle Station and accessible only to people on skis. Spectator interest was limited at best.

"[The Lowell Thomas Classic] attracted the premier amateur racers in the country," says Anderson, "but it only attracted the participants. The locals weren't interested, and as a result, there weren't many spectators."

There were also glitches to contend with. Anderson recalls using the Skier's Subway on at least one occasion. "The gondola was off the track due to wind. We used the mine [train] to transport [the competitors to] the race."

The gondola figures into another race story as well. There was a big race in the late 1960s on Thaynes, near the top of Thaynes Canyon, that included Jean-Claude Killy, fresh from his triple-gold-medal performance at the 1968 Olympics, as well as 1964 Olympic medalists Billy Kidd and Jimmie Heuga from the

ABOVE: CBS BROADCASTING LEGEND LOWELL
THOMAS WAS AN EARLY PARK CITY VISITOR. HE
LOANED HIS NAME TO AN EARLY RACE SERIES. LEFT:
AS PARK CITY'S REPUTATION GREW, CELEBRITIES
LIKE JILL ST. JOHN STARRED IN FUND-RAISING
CELEBRITY RACES LIKE THE JILL ST. JOHN-MASSON
CELEBRITY SKI INVITATIONAL IN 1976.

U.S. Team. As Killy exited the gondola at the top, the gondola attendant—a miner transferred to United Park City Mines' recreation division—spoke his oft-repeated mantra, "Pick up your skis and exit, please." Killy missed the instructions or misunderstood them, so his race skis, still nestled in the rack on the outside of the gondola, continued around the bullwheel and

headed down the mountain again. The great Killy steamed for the next 44 minutes until his skis came back up. "He's no better than any other skier and not half as smart," the gondola attendant muttered to fellow gondola workers.

Any race with Jean-Claude Killy is an important race, but this was nothing compared with the level of racing that Craig Badami would bring to the mountain in the 1980s. The red-haired, freckled-faced son of Nick Badami was a born promoter who turned the ski-racing world upside down and transformed Park City in the process. "He was enthusiastic 26 hours a day," his father recalls. "His expression was, 'When in doubt, go skiing.'"

C.B. went skiing around the world, attending World Cup races throughout Europe and attending the Winter Olympics,

THE HERCULEAN EFFORT TO STAGE THE FIRST
WORLD CUP REQUIRED WINCHING SNOWCATS UP
AND DOWN USING A D-8 CAT (RIGHT) AS A RIDGE-
TOP ANCHOR POINT. ABOVE RIGHT: A SNOWCAT
ATTACHMENT TO PUNCH HOLES THROUGH THE
SNOW. THE HOSES (ABOVE THE EQUIPMENT) FILLED
THE HOLES WITH WATER TO HARDEN THE SURFACE.

observing how races were organized, how they were staged and how the athletes and fans were treated, and learning what went right and what was wrong. Along the way he built relationships with FIS racing officials.

Park City had already begun shedding its "Easy Acres" label with the expansion into Jupiter Bowl. "Next we wanted to position Park City on a world-class basis," Nick Badami says. "[To do that] we needed world-class racing, and Craig went out to get it."

European resorts dominated the World Cup schedule, and Europeans controlled the FIS. Very few American resorts were awarded regular World Cup races, and what races were held in the U.S. were always in the spring. Badami saw his opportunity in the spring of 1985 when another resort backed out of a World Cup race with just weeks to spare. Park City had eight weeks to do what its employees had never done before, and they had to do it in a way FIS officials could not ignore.

For one thing, they had to prepare the slopes the way the

World Cup racers and officials liked them—rock hard. After a season of deep snow and only light recreational use, the Men's GS trail off Ski Team Ridge needed some serious grooming. But the run was too steep for a snowcat.

"You're going to do what?" snow grooming chief Brian Strait asked incredulously. His boss, Phil Jones, had just proposed driving a D-8 Caterpillar (not designed for use on snow) from the resort base all the way up Ski Team Ridge to the top of the racecourse to use as an anchor. He figured they could attach a winch to the cat and run a cable through it to two snowcats. One would groom *up* while another groomed *down*, with the 40-ton D-8

MEN'S GS ON SKI TEAM RIDGE, READY FOR RACING. THE RACES MOVED TO EAGLE ARENA IN 1993.

anchoring the jerry-rigged yo-yo from the top. The weight of the snowcat going down would help pull the snowcat going up, Jones reasoned. Both snowcats had to be in sync, and after some trial and error, two Thiokol 2100 snowcats were yo-yoing nicely. "It was one of the craziest things we've ever done," Strait laughs.

While Jones and Strait prepared the mountain, Craig Badami's head spun with innovative ideas for putting on the race. From what he'd seen at most European World Cup races, skiers and spectators showed up, stood around, raced and went home. He wanted people to have an experience. He wanted to throw a party and invite the world. By the time the party was over, he figured, everyone in the world would know where Park City Ski Area was. He packed a year's worth of planning and organization into two frenetic months.

"Craig was a huge San Francisco 49ers and Joe Montana fan," his protégé and friend Charlie Lansche remembers. "He used football analogies, [and he] wasn't afraid to throw the long pass."

Mark Menlove was working for the Park City Chamber of Commerce at the time and pitched in to help promote the event.

THE INAUGURAL 1985 WORLD CUP. THE RACE
ATTRACTED THE BIGGEST CROWD EVER TO WATCH A
WORLD CUP RACE IN THE UNITED STATES.

"There was never a sense we couldn't do this. If Craig said we
could do it, everybody believed we could."

"Everybody at the resort had their own picture of what the
World Cup would be," Strait laughs. "And Craig's picture was
always *at least* 100 times bigger than any other single picture."
Soon resort workers were building a full-size stage and erecting
enough tents to host gourmet VIP lunches between the two runs
of racing each day. "It was mind-boggling how much stuff had to
be moved up the hill, but it all happened," says Strait.

The March 1985 World Cup was a slalom race, with
women the first day and men the second. After an advertising blitz in Salt Lake City, ski racing was suddenly what
Utahns wanted to see. Twelve thousand of them showed up,
making the grueling hike up to the finish line or higher. The
stage rocked with live music at nine o'clock in the morning
before the first run at 10. Temperatures climbed into the 50s,

and the race went off before the largest crowd ever to see a
World Cup ski race in the U.S.

During the break between runs, as the VIPs lined up for
a fancy hot lunch, the music kicked in, with C.B. himself on
stage playing blues harmonica with the local band Johnny and

ABOVE: ERIKA HESS OF SWITZERLAND WON THE WOMEN'S GS WORLD CUP DURING ITS FIRST TWO YEARS AT PARK CITY. CRAIG BADAMI CONGRATULATED HER, AND LATER RENAMED THE MEN'S GS RUN "ERIKA'S GOLD." LEFT: WORLD CUP RACES WENT WAY BEYOND RACING, SERVING GOURMET LUNCHES BETWEEN RACES.

the Rockers. In the afternoon, Swiss racer Erika Hess took the women's gold. Rock and roll cranked up again after the podium ceremony, and that evening fireworks and a free blues concert lit up the eyes and ears of everyone in town. In later World Cups, the entertainment included free concerts by Bonnie Raitt, America, the Nitty Gritty Dirt Band and Joe Walsh (although Walsh played only two songs before announcing, "I gotta pee," and then staggering off the stage, never to return).

"The amount of energy that Craig personally brought was just incredible," Strait says. "It was truly a party." Dominant American World Cup racer Tamara McKinney, sponsored by Park City Ski Area, had her own description. "It's a rock concert where a ski race breaks out in the middle of it." Day two brought a second day of temperatures in the 50s, playful snowball fights among the fans, the "wave" rippling through the crowd, more rock and roll, more food and, in between, a world-class World Cup ski race.

The success of that first World Cup earned Park City a

TAMARA MCKINNEY, SKIING UNDER PARK CITY SPONSORSHIP, SHOWING THE SPEED THAT MADE HER AMERICA'S TOP RACER OF HER GENERATION.

repeat performance on the same weekend the next year. With more lead time, Phil Jones ordered a paved road built in the summer from the base up the hill to the finish line. By March the next year, when it came time to haul the equipment up the hill, the road was hopelessly buried under a season's worth of snow and couldn't be found. Attempts to dig down to it created a mess in the middle of the most important trail off the mountain at the end of the day. But the problem remained: how to get a huge TV production truck up to the finish line, 470 vertical feet and two thirds of a mile from the parking lot.

Jones and Strait came up with another scheme. "We decided to pull the truck (cab and all) with snowcats," Strait chuckles. "Two or three wouldn't budge the truck, so we just got more snowcats. It was a hell of a line of snowcats all hooked together tugging on that truck." Eventually they connected enough of them to get the job done. In future years, they would find a way to use the paved road.

The second World Cup featured ladies only. Erika Hess turned in a repeat slalom performance, taking the gold back to Switzerland. Resort management renamed the Men's GS trail, calling it Erika's Gold.

TOP: 1995. PARK CITY SKI AREA PULLED OFF THE AMERICA'S OPENING WORLD CUP WITHOUT A FLAKE OF NATURAL SNOW. IT LOOKED GOOD ON ESPN, EXCEPT FOR THE WIDE SHOTS. ABOVE: THE BAND "AMERICA" KICKED OFF THE WEEKEND WITH A FREE MAIN STREET CONCERT. RIGHT: CRAIG BADAMI CLOWNS WITH SKI TEAM RACER PAM FLETCHER.

Those two years of successful World Cups put Park City on the map of international ski racing and let the world know that the Utah resort could put on a great ski race and party at the end of the season. But as successful as the races were, they didn't help Craig Badami get the message to recreational skiers that Park City was a great place to ski earlier in the season.

USSAUF

ABOVE, LEFT: RESORT PUBLIC RELATIONS DIRECTOR
MARK MENLOVE EMCEES A WORLD CUP, WITH AVIS
AND NICK BADAMI. THE AVIS BADAMI CUP WENT TO
THE SKIER WHO ACCUMALTED THE MOST POINTS
OVER TWO DAYS OF RACING. LEFT: HARALD
SCHOENHAAR'S FIRST U.S. SKI TEAM JOB WAS TO
LOAD A RENTAL TRUCK AND MOVE THE OFFICES FROM
DENVER TO PARK CITY. COACHING CAME LATER.

Now he lobbied hard for an early-season race, eventually con-
vincing ski-racing officials that the season could open in November
in Park City because of the resort's snowmaking. The FIS agreed to
open the World Cup season in Park City on November 30, 1986.
The women came to race a giant slalom and slalom on Payday, where
ample snow guns could guarantee coverage.

C.B. promoted it as "America's Opening," and once again ski
racing and rock and roll dominated the weekend. Now when the
stories of the races went out, skiers worldwide knew that Park
City, Utah, was open for early season skiing.

FIS scheduling conflicts prevented Park City from opening
the World Cup the next two years, so Badami switched to pro ski
racing, again on Payday and again in November. The timing was

PHIL AND STEVE MAHRE TURNED PRO THE YEAR
PARK CITY TURNED TO PRO RACING. THEY SHUNNED
THE PAYDAY LIFT IN FAVOR OF WALKING UP
BETWEEN RUNS. THE PRO FORMAT OFFERED TERRAIN
FEATURES, LIKE JUMPS AND HEAD-TO-HEAD RACING.

perfect. America's most decorated World Cup skiers, Phil and
Steve Mahre, turned pro that year (1988), guaranteeing big
crowds for the professional head-to-head format.

"Rather than taking the lift up Payday [between runs], [the
Mahres] would put their skis on their shoulders and walk back
up," Menlove remembers with awe. Whether it psyched up the
brothers or psyched out their competitors is hard to figure, but
Steve Mahre won the race.

During a pause between runs, Austrian Franz Weber put on
a speed skiing exhibition. Race announcer Jack Turner told the
crowd that the Park City police had provided a radar gun so that

THE WORLD CUP SLALOM FINISH AT THE BASE OF WILLY'S RUN, BEFORE THE MOVE TO EAGLE ARENA.

Weber's speed could be tracked as he tucked Payday top to bottom. When nobody could find the radar gun, Turner grabbed a portable drill used for setting racecourses, pulled out the oversize bit, pointed the drill at Weber as if it were a radar gun, and said, "Ladies and gentlemen: Franz Weber, 45 miles an hour...58, 63. Ladies and gentlemen, 73 miles an hour here on Payday run!"

"I didn't know I was going that fast," Weber said later. "It didn't feel that fast!"

The World Cup returned in November 1989 with GS and slalom races to open both the men's and women's seasons. Badami booked the band America for a free street dance at the bottom of Main Street. Once more the Park City race crew carted stages, trucks, tents and food up to the race hill. (The race trail formerly called Women's GS had been renamed Willy's Run in honor of former U.S. Ski Team Alpine coach and long-time University of Denver ski coach Willy Schaeffler, who had died the previous year.)

The first day's racing was flawless. As America played for the street dance that night, the snow started falling in big, wet flakes. The awning draped over the band drooped ever lower as America ran through its playlist and the happy crowd danced. As the concert ended, Craig Badami came on stage and said, "We're gonna shoot off $35,000 worth of fireworks into this snow. We'll see what happens!" The fireworks exploded through the falling flakes, turning them red, blue, green and purple.

It would be the last memory many would have of Craig Badami.

The storm dumped too much snow on the racecourse, and there wasn't enough time to restore it to the rock-hard racing surface that the FIS required. Postponement for a day wasn't possible, because the World Cup traveling circus had to move on to the next venue.

After all that work, Park City Ski Area employees were seriously disappointed. But as always, Craig Badami was there cheering everyone up. "Think of it this way," he said. "The word goes out that the World Cup was canceled because Park City had too much snow! This is great! You can't buy that kind of publicity!"

ALL READY THE NIGHT BEFORE THE FIRST AMERICA'S OPENING, ON WOMEN'S GS IN 1986. THE NEON SIGN WAS ONE MORE CRAIG BADAMI TOUCH.

When the weather cleared, race workers began taking everything down. A six-passenger Alouette helicopter that had been used the previous week to ferry equipment up the mountain was now employed to bring it down. If there was one thing Craig Badami was passionate about (in addition to his son, Nicholas, his parents, skiing, the San Francisco 49ers, the U.S. Ski Team and music), it was riding in helicopters. He took annual heli-ski trips to the Canadian Rockies with a half-dozen Park City ski buddies, a group that became known among heli-skiers as the "Park City Wrecking Crew" for its boisterous behavior. On the Tuesday after the canceled race, he hopped into the Alouette's left front seat for the ride back up to the top of the race hill. Five passengers and the pilot were aboard. Just after lifting off from the lower parking lot, the dangling cargo cable snagged a corner of a ski waxing trailer. The helicopter climbed until the cable grew taut. The sudden resistance yanked the ship sideways. Then the cable broke free of the trailer and slingshotted up into the rotor, shattering it. The Alouette fell hard onto First Time ski run in the Three Kings area.

Onlookers swarmed in. Ski patrollers arrived fast and went to work. The pilot and four of the passengers were critically injured. Mark Menlove ran to the scene. A patrolman looked up at him. "Craig's gone," he said.

Word rocketed through town, from the grocery store to city hall to Main Street. Phones rang as friends spread the word. In a one-industry town, the death of the industry leader hurts everyone personally. The World Cup celebration that had come to signal the joyous start of the ski season ended in unspeakable tragedy. Grief dominated every aspect of Park City life that day, and for months after.

At the memorial service, held on the resort plaza, there was a 21-explosion salute of avalanche charges by the ski patrol, a release of pink and white balloons and white fireworks against a blue Utah sky.

C.B. would have loved it.

THE 1986 STREET DANCE AT THE BASE OF MAIN STREET. FREE RESORT-SPONSORED HEADLINER
CONCERTS HAVE BECOME A REGULAR PART OF THE WORLD CUP PACKAGE IN PARK CITY.

A Day with C.B.

Footsteps in the hall. Loud, heavy footsteps that the people in the ticket office below would complain about. Again. From the sound, I knew he was wearing his tan alligator-skin cowboy boots, his favorites. I also knew what would come next. Halfway down the hall, his raspy voice: "Charlie! Mark! In my office, NOW!" It could have just as easily been Robbie or Sheri or Jodi he bellowed at, but that day he was excited about a powerful machine in the parking lot, and so it was the boys, as he liked to call us, whom he summoned.

helicopter waited. He introduced us to the pilot, Lynn. Though they had just met, he treated Lynn like an old friend. The people he liked, he liked immediately. And if he liked you, whether you were a rock star, a senator or an unemployed ski bum, he pulled you along into his inner circle and shared whatever he had with you. He once told me his philosophy about choosing friends was summed up in a single line from a Grateful Dead song: "What I want to know is, are you kind?"

After the short helicopter ride, C.B. surveyed the scene from a

Craig Badami, "The P.T. Barnum of American ski racing," at right with racer Tamara McKinney, who reached the top of the World Cup circuit.

Never mind that we were busy with important things: writing press releases and finalizing group sales contracts. When he was excited about a new idea, a new toy or a new interest, all of which came often to him, he demanded that we drop what we were doing so he could wind us up with his ideas and assignments and send us off like spinning tops. It was part of the fun and frustration of working for Craig Badami, a red-haired, freckle-nosed bundle of energy who did everything in a bigger, better, grander, louder, faster fashion than the rest of the world.

That day's assignment was easy. The six-passenger Alouette helicopter he'd hired for the week to shuttle equipment and VIPs to the World Cup race site on Willy's Run had just arrived, and he wanted us to fly with him to the finish area to check on the readiness of the race facilities. So, with press releases half finished and sales contracts unsigned, we put on our jackets and trailed behind him to the parking lot where the

wooden platform above the Willy's Run finish area: Massive food tents where gourmet lunches would be served, rows of sturdy bleacher seating, and his favorite touch, a huge stage with a full concert sound system. Rock bands between runs, fireworks, halftime entertainment, celebrities like Wilt Chamberlain and Bonnie Raitt on hand—it was all part of his grand scheme to make ski racing exciting to an American public disinterested in any sport that didn't involve a ball and at the same time to put Park City on the map with European skiers who followed the World Cup religiously. His innovations worked: Skiers in America and Europe took notice.

But expanding market share was only part of C.B.'s motivation. He was a ski-racing junkie. He adored the sport and the athletes who participated in it and wanted to do whatever he could to give them a proper showcase.

C.B. rubbed his hands together. "Man, I'm nervous all of a sudden," he said.

"Yeah," said Charlie. "We've never opened both the men's and women's circuits at the same time. A lot of pressure."

But C.B. didn't seem to hear. His eyes had that crazy glint they took on when his brain was racing. "I mean, I've played for a few hundred people in bars, but 10,000 people.... There'll be 10,000 people listening to us play."

Charlie and I exchanged an understanding grin. That was it. One of C.B.'s many passions was blues harmonica. He'd scheduled the local band he often gigged with, Johnny and the Rockers, to play several times during the four days of World Cup festivities. It was only natural that as ringmaster of this party, he would command center stage. Just 37 years old, he had already been dubbed by *Ski Racing* magazine the P.T. Barnum of skiing for his showmanship and unconventional approach to ski-area marketing.

Back in the helicopter, C.B. asked Lynn to fly to the top of the course and then swoop down low following the contours of Willy's Run. Next we boomed down along Ski Team Ridge and Craig chattered in rapid-fire staccato about the permanent race stadium he wanted to build near the resort base. We circled over the rest of the resort—to the top of Jupiter Peak, the expert's paradise that was Craig's first expansion after the Badamis bought the resort, then beyond to 10420, an even higher peak that he had his eye on. He rattled on excitedly about future plans, not as a businessman looking to increase his assets, but with the pure joy of a child in charge of building his own playground. This was his kingdom. He loved it.

Six days later, after a wildly successful America's Opening, C.B. climbed back aboard the helicopter with some of the crew and within moments was dead.

Images of the crash scene and the aftermath still haunt me. But the image that comes into clearest focus, still crisp after 14 years, is from three days before the crash. An image of C.B. at his last World Cup. I see him there at center stage blowing wicked soulful harp, red hair bouncing, hands cupping both microphone and harmonica, cheeks puffed out, eyes shining like some wild beat poet, alligator-skin boots stomping the stage. And 10,000 people cheering him on. —Mark Menlove

—Mark Menlove was communications director for Park City Ski Area during the early World Cup years. Now he is a Park City–based writer.

EAGLE ARENA CONSTRUCTION IN THE SUMMER OF 1993. C.B.'S RUN ON THE LEFT, PICABO'S IN THE CENTER, AND A PRACTICE FREESTYLE RUN ON THE RIGHT. SNOWMAKING AIR AND WATER LINES ARE IN THE PROCESS OF BEING BURIED.

EPILOGUE

In 1991, the FIS agreed to hold annual America's Opening races in Park City, a tradition that continues to this day. The racers loved coming to Park City, and other race organizers took note. "Now [all the World Cup] races have VIP facilities and meals," says Hank Tauber, a former FIS vice president. "Park City got that whole idea going."

Former U.S. Ski Team alpine coach Harald Schoenhaar says his friends at his home ski resort in Germany, where World Cup races were also held, once complained to him, "We're not coming to Park City anymore, because you and your Park City crew put too much pressure on us. We have to build tents in the middle of winter!"

Major World Cup venues in Europe have adopted some of the Park City innovations, but U.S. Ski Team vice president Tom Kelly, a frequent traveler to World Cup events, says it's not universal. "Craig recognized that ski racing, to be successful, needs to be entertainment. It can't just be people coming down the mountain."

It was apparent early on that the racing trails at the top of Ski Team Ridge, while ideal as racecourses, were not logistically or spectator friendly. Even before Craig Badami's death, he and others were looking lower on the mountain for a place to build a racing venue closer to the resort base, where trucks could drive into position, and fans could hop off busses and walk a short, flat distance to the races.

The ideal place turned out to be on the same Ski Team Ridge as Willy's Run and Erika's Gold, but farther down, near the Three Kings area. "Craig spotted early on that it had to be accessible, it had to hold a lot of spectators, and it had to be available to others for racing, like ski clubs and teams," Nick Badami recalls. "Hank Tauber and Harald Schoenhaar helped him lay out the courses; they walked it a million times." Karen Korfanta, Park City Ski Area's director of racing, was also a key figure in the trail design.

The design called for three separate runs served by a new chairlift going over the middle section to provide a midway exit station for the shorter technical events like slalom and freestyle moguls. "The best thing about it is you have different racecourses that all end in the same area, where you can build one stadium," says Schoenhaar, now retired, who splits his time between Germany and Park City.

When America's Opening arrived on November 25, 1994, it debuted in a new venue, a racing arena away from the main ski area and dedicated to ski training and the best ski racing in the world.

But what to call it? At the Badami family home in Lake Tahoe, eagles were a frequent, welcome sight. And eagles seemed to appear in the vicinity of the race arena every fall around World Cup time.

Eagle Race Arena was ready for the best in the world. ⋏

AMERICA'S OPENING TODAY. THE ROAR OF THE CROWD GETS LOUDER AS RACERS DROP DOWN GOTCHA FACE, THROUGH THE GRADE, AND ONTO C.B.'S FACE AND THE FINISH ARENA.

CHAPTER 7

THE ALPINE HEART
OF 2002

It was huge—14.8 feet high, 55 feet wide and 525 feet long. It took crews months to stockpile enough machine-made snow to make it and a full week to carve it into the perfect shape. In the end it stayed up only a few days. Then, overnight, course workers obliterated every trace of it. But during its few glorious days in the Eagle Race Arena during the Olympic Winter Games of 2002, the Olympic Superpipe earned a place in sports history.

It was Day Two of the 19th Olympic Winter Games, and Park City Mountain Resort's first day on the worldwide Olympic stage. More than 16,000 fans sat in a temporary stadium or stood on tiers of snow cut into a hillside. The stadium at the base of the Eagle lift looked much like Craig Badami had envisioned it years earlier—a quarter-circle-shaped stadium wrapping the finish line for both snowboarding and skiing events. On hand was the largest crowd ever to watch a snowboarding event live. In addition to the 16,000 spectators were members of the press, volunteers, officials and assorted other VIPs (like snowboard legend Jake Burton), bringing the total attendance to around 20,000. Plus several hundred million more who were watching on television around the globe.

THE EAGLE SUPERPIPE, FULL GRANDSTANDS, AND THE BIG SHOW. THE XIX
OLYMPIC WINTER GAMES AT EAGLE ARENA. ABOVE: KELLY CLARK KICKS
THINGS OFF LIGHTNING FAST WITH THE GOLD ON DAY TWO.

ABOVE: KELLY CLARK GETTING AMPLITUDE BEFORE THE PUMPED UP CROWD. RIGHT: THE WOMEN HALFPIPE MEDALISTS CELEBRATE, (LEFT TO RIGHT) SILVER MEDALIST DORIANE VIDAL OF FRANCE, GOLD MEDALIST KELLY CLARK OF THE USA AND BRONZE MEDALIST FABIENNE REUTELER OF SWITZERLAND.

The venue was all dressed up for its moment on the world stage. Fencing was erected with blue netting printed with the five Olympic rings, the Salt Lake 2002 snowflake logo and the official Games slogan, "Light the Fire Within." The back of the temporary stadium was draped with a 10-story-high banner showing a GS ski racer in action. When you add fans bundled in colorful ski clothing, waving flags and banners, and ringing all sorts of cowbells and other noisemakers, this day, February 10, 2002, was like the Super Bowl of snowboarding, a sport making only its second appearance in the Olympic Games.

"I knew what I needed to do was go all out, because I knew I would regret it if I didn't," Kelly Clark, an 18-year-old snowboarder from Mount Snow, Vermont, told the *Boston Globe* afterward. Poised at the top of the Superpipe, Clark was a picture of concentration. For her public music she had selected "Welcome

to the Jungle" by Guns N' Roses, and now it was blasting from the public-address speakers as she prepared to go to work in the pipe. But what she heard through her portable mini disc player was "This Is Growing Up" by Blink 182.

In just her second year on the U.S. Snowboard Team, Clark had nailed her first run in the finals with all the right tricks and

KELLY CLARK, EIGHTEEN YEARS OLD AND ON TOP OF THE SNOWBOARDING WORLD.

huge amplitude off the walls. She was in position to medal after her first run, but what color would it be? The second run left no question. The heavily American crowd roared loud enough that Clark heard it over her cranked-up soundtrack. Every trick went perfectly. On the second day of competition, America had its first gold medal of the 2002 Games.

The idea for bringing the Olympics to Utah actually started in the mid 1960s. *Salt Lake Tribune* publisher Jack Gallivan was at a small dinner party at the governor's mansion with Governor Calvin Rampton and retired general Max Rich, head of the Salt Lake Chamber of Commerce. After dinner the men retired to the basement for a drink, and Gallivan started bemoaning the fact that Park City's new ski resort was losing money because it didn't have the cash to get the word out that Utah had great skiing.

"Why don't we try to get the Winter Olympics, to generate some publicity?" Rich suggested. The governor and Gallivan thought the idea outlandish. "Good God, Max, what if we win?" Governor Rampton asked, knowing Utah was in no position to pull off the Games, especially since they were invariably money-losers for host cities at that time. But Rich wouldn't give up. "Don't worry. We don't have a chance of winning," he assured them, and then predicted that Utah would reap millions of dollars in free publicity just by being in the competition to host the Games.

A last-minute campaign for the Winter Olympics was launched, and soon Olympic boosters were off to Rome to meet with the delegates of the International Olympic Committee (IOC). Salt Lakers had pictures, bid specifications and maps ready to answer any question. A few IOC bigwigs, like King Constantine of Greece, were impressed, which struck fear in the

bid leaders. "If we win," Rampton kidded Gallivan, "we're going to have to mortgage the Cathedral of the Madeleine," the center of Utah Catholicism and the church built largely through the contributions of Gallivan's uncle, the Silver King millionaire Thomas Kearns.

"I told Cal I had another building in mind down the street," Gallivan recalled years later at a banquet honoring early Olympic boosters, referring to the Mormon Temple of Rampton's faith.

The bid failed but Utah's name got out there as a ski destination. Sapporo, Japan, won the 1972 Games. "And Sapporo," Rampton chuckled years later, "lost millions!"

But by the 1980s, Utah was tired of playing second fiddle to the Colorado ski juggernaut next door. Its resorts did well enough but were far underutilized. The 1984 Los Angeles Olympics had proven that the Games could be marketed to corporate America and actually make money for the host city. An Olympic host-city designation would raise Utah's profile instantly, and the construction of highways, venues, hotels and everything else associated with the world's biggest sporting event would stimulate Utah's sluggish economy. "A rising tide lifts all ships" was a favored expression at the time in landlocked Utah.

With L.A.'s success, every American city now wanted the Games. It was up to the United States Olympic Committee (USOC) to pick its candidate city. Salt Lake lost the U.S. rights to bid for the 1994 games to Anchorage, a two-time bidder. Two years later, it won the rights to bid for the 1998 games by beating Anchorage, which by then was a two-time IOC bid loser. Denver and the Reno-Tahoe area were the other bidders.

But the 1998 nomination came with a price. The USOC wanted more training facilities for American athletes, so it required the U.S. candidate city to promise to build venues up front, even before the IOC decided which city to select for the 1998 games.

Utah Olympic boosters went to work, getting a statewide referendum passed that channeled $59 million from sales tax revenue into a speed skating oval, a ski jumping complex and a bobsled and luge track. It would be difficult to find a state more conservative with its money than Utah, yet Utah voters agreed to invest in these multimillion-dollar facilities with no guarantee that the state would land the Olympics.

The next step was an elaborate international campaign. To many it seemed doomed from the start. Atlanta had won the 1996 summer Games. To award back-to-back Olympics to two American cities seemed so remote that many experts told Salt

ABOVE: SOARING ON THE K-120 AT UTAH OLYMPIC PARK. ABOVE, RIGHT: U.S. SKI AND SNOWBOARD TEAM CEO BILL MAROLT CARRIES THE TORCH DOWN MAIN STREET. RIGHT: UTAHNS WERE URGED TO DECORATE THEIR HOMES FOR THE GAMES.

Lake to not even bother with a campaign. Still, with an army of volunteers who made it a point to know every IOC member's spouse's birthday, the committee campaigned to win, and in 1991 came within an astonishing four votes, losing to Nagano, Japan for the 1998 games.

Two years after the Nagano loss, the Utah campaigners had one last shot. The USOC had promised to let the bid city that built training facilities have two tries before the IOC. The pressure was enormous. The practice facilities were already under construction. The campaign was more wide open this time. The Salt Lake Bid Committee was more generous with their entertaining and gifting to IOC delegates. The committee could also point to the seriousness of their bid by escorting IOC members to nearly completed venues for ski jumping and bobsledding at the Utah Winter Sports Park (later renamed the Utah Olympic Park) near Kimball Junction outside Park City, and they could

point out Salt Lake's long history of not giving up. The true nature of the gifting would only come to the surface later in a bribery scandal that rocked the Olympic movement.

This time around, Salt Lake was the front-runner. It stayed that way. Against three other bid cities—Ostersund, Sweden; Sion, Switzerland; and Quebec City, Canada—Salt Lake won an overwhelming majority of votes on the first ballot. In Salt Lake, a

OPENING CEREMONIES AT RICE-ECCLES STADIUM ON THE UNIVERSITY OF UTAH CAMPUS. THE FOOTBALL FIELD BECAME A SKATING RINK.

huge crowd at the City-County Building downtown watched the announcement by IOC President Juan Antonio Samaranch in Budapest. On the words "Salt Lake City," the crowd erupted—a picture carried around the world that night.

The morning after Kelly Clark delivered the first American gold, it was the men's turn on the Superpipe. The Salt Lake Olympic Organizing Committee (SLOC) and Park City Mountain Resort (PCMR) planners had prepared for years for bad weather and were ready to turn out an army to clear race courses of new snow and dig out the Superpipe. But Day Three of the Games was just a perfect as Day Two—in fact, more perfect because of what was about to unfold.

"There was a lot of chatter about the Americans early on,

that maybe they were the best in the world," says Charlie Lansche, the former resort spokesman and protégé of Craig Badami. Lansche was volunteering as chief of press at Eagle Race Arena, with his old colleague Mark Menlove as his assistant. "There was this buzz."

After the morning qualifying round, four Americans were poised in medal position: Tommy Czeschin, Ross Powers, Danny Kass and J.J. Thomas. The judges were rewarding the big jumps—known as "amplitude"—and all the Americans were flying off the Superpipe walls with near perfect tricks. The psyched crowd started smelling a sweep, and chants of "USA! USA! USA!" rocked the stands.

Ross Powers felt it at the top of the pipe. "The weather was amazing," Powers says. "The temperature held firm so we could

ABOVE: DANNY KASS WORKING THE PIPE. RIGHT: ROSS POWERS GETTING AMPLITUDE. BOTH WOULD MEDAL ON U.S. SNOWBOARDING'S BIGGEST DAY.

carry speed. It was the biggest crowd we'd ever had. My mom, brother, cousins and friends were all there."

In the final round, Powers recalls, he landed his "biggest backside air" ever and "landed a frontside air nearly as big." Then came a McTwist, an upside-down 540, followed by back-to-back 720s, a stalefish grab, a backside 360 and a switch McTwist. Powers' amplitude reached 18 to 20 feet above the pipe's rim, which was nearly 15 feet high to start with, putting him more than 30 feet up.

Powers' name went to the top of the leader board and stayed there. Danny Kass's name came in under his, followed by J.J. Thomas'.

"It was electric, incredible. It sent shivers up my spine." PCMR mountain operations vice president Brian Strait remembers the moment like it was yesterday. His crews had made the snow and pushed it into position for SLOC's pipe builder Pat Malendoski to shape into perfection. Seeing the sweep, and knowing that his PCMR employees set the stage, "It was the pinnacle—nothing else compares to it—nothing even comes close!"

Jake Burton, who for years had campaigned against allowing snowboarding in the Olympics because he felt the Games would take the edge off the sport's vibrant, outlaw image, turned to Lansche in the VIP area and said, "This is the best snowboarding event I've ever seen in my life. It's the best snowboarding event that's ever taken place on the planet!"

"There was a lot of good karma in Park City during the Games," says Lansche. The good karma spilled onto Park City's

THE USA MEN'S SNOWBOARD SWEEP. LEFT TO RIGHT: THOMAS, BRONZE; POWERS, GOLD; KASS, SILVER.

Main Street that day and every day during the Olympics. Park City town leaders had been planning for these 17 days of Olympic competition for eight years. Observation teams had gone to all summer and winter Olympics to look, listen and learn. They realized early on that competition inside the fence is just one part of the Olympic experience. After seeing the foot traffic on the main thoroughfare of Norway's Lillehammer during the 1994 Games, they banished cars from Park City's Main Street area during the 2002 Games. The only real way into town was on SLOC's mass transportation system. When venues were "loading" and "unloading," buses borrowed from cities and counties and transit districts nationwide rolled into town from outlying park-and-ride lots at the rate of one per minute. It was stunning to see an Orange County (California) transit bus, followed by one with a flashing message board proclaiming "Cleveland Rocks." (On the streets of Salt Lake, the new light rail system was running its cars, plus bigger ones labeled DART—for Dallas Area Rapid Transit.)

Arriving pedestrians on Main Street found a street lined with banners and food booths. Propane warming fires sponsored by local residents and businesses served as informal gathering places, where a visiting Austrian might strike up a conversation with an Englishman and a Parkite. Pins and handshakes would be exchanged, further kindling the Olympic spirit. Official SLOC entertainers, from singing ladies with teacup hats to cast members of the Games' opening ceremonies, mingled on the street. Cops walking the beat were as likely to come from Boston or Philadelphia as from Park City. Fire and paramedic units were beefed up with men and women from New York City, Michigan and just about anywhere.

The U.S. Olympic Team's "Roots 2002" berets were the fashion hit of the Games. At its peak, the wait time to squeeze into the tiny Roots souvenir store on Park City's Main Street would run two hours. Lucky customers coming out with the prized berets could instantly sell them to those in the back of the line for more than double the $20 they paid, but most wouldn't part with

them despite pleas to give them up for a quick profit.

Every afternoon, the Budweiser Clydesdales pulled their beer wagon down Main Street, the teamster riding the brake the whole way. Every evening, in the parking lot above the Wasatch Brew Pub, bands cranked up. After the music stopped, SLOC showed emotional thrill-of-victory, agony-of-defeat videos on big screen TVs, followed by fireworks.

On some days, transportation planners shuddered at the thought of transporting 20,000 people to Utah Olympic Park, 20,000 more to Park City Mountain Resort or Deer Valley Resort (home of freestyle and slalom ski events) and 20,000 on Highway 40 to Soldier Hollow in the Heber Valley 15 miles away, home of cross-country and biathlon competitions. With nearly perfect weather every day, years of planning paid off, and no spectator could complain of transportation snafus denying them their moment to witness Olympic glory.

Meanwhile, back at the Eagle Race Arena, Brian Strait's mountain operations crews now had to turn the area into a venue for parallel giant slalom snowboarding. One hour after the U.S. men's sweep, Strait's snowcats were pushing the carefully sculpted sides of the Superpipe down into the trough. "I wasn't excited to see it come down after the results we had," he

recalls, but the next race was just three days away, and the racers needed practice time.

The PCMR crews had rehearsed this turnaround the previous year when Park City hosted a Superpipe test event. That time it took a day and a half to complete. Now they stepped it up, taking care to pack the snow so the snowboard racers would not detect a change in snow conditions as they dropped from the top half of the course onto the newly groomed section at the bottom.

"We did it overnight, and it was ready for race practice when the sun came up," Strait brags, with obvious pride in his employees. "There were definitely some anxious moments, but the snow firmed up nicely."

The qualifying rounds for both men and women came off without delay. On February 15, the crowd was back, big as ever, and American fans had something to cheer about again, as the bronze medal went to Aspen rider Chris Klug. Even in the third position, Klug became the instant symbol of Olympic triumph.

Two years earlier, his liver failing from the same rare liver disease that killed football great Walter Payton of the Chicago Bears, Klug was unsure whether he'd live long enough to see the Olympics, let alone compete in them. For 72 days he waited on

ALPINE SNOWBOARDING ACTION. THE HEAD-TO-HEAD FORMAT OF THE MEN'S PARALLEL GIANT SLALOM MADE IT A SPECTATOR FAVORITE.

A TRIUMPH OF WILL AND MODERN MEDICINE: CHRIS KLUG COMES BACK FROM A NEAR-FATAL DISEASE TO CAPTURE BRONZE IN THE PARALLEL GS.

the liver transplant list. With Salt Lake 2002 just 18 months away, he got his new liver and started rebuilding his body, getting used to the transplant drugs and a new chance at life and his Olympic dreams.

So far everything was looking good. In the first seven days of Olympic competition, five Americans, all snowboarders, had brought home medals, two of them gold, and all of them at Park City's Eagle Race Arena. U.S. Ski and Snowboard Team CEO Bill Marolt was already halfway to his oft-stated goal to bring home 10 medals at his hometown Olympics.

Marolt, a member of the historic 1964 U.S. Olympic Team (with Billy Kidd, Jimmie Heuga and Buddy Werner), had been alpine director of the team during the glory days of the early '80s when Phil Mahre and Tamara McKinney were World Cup champions. In 1984 he became athletic director of his alma mater, the University of Colorado, where he learned as much as led. "Bill McCartney was the football coach at the time. He always said if you're afraid to set goals and tack them on the wall, you're not committed."

McCartney took the CU Buffalos to the National Championships in 1990, and Marolt learned something about goal setting. "I got here [to the Ski and Snowboard Team] and we talked about goals—that they have to be achievable, but they've got to be a stretch. Ten medals was a stretch goal, it was

Olympic Legacies

When Salt Lake 2002 bid leader Tom Welch and his assistant, Dave Johnson, set out a second time to win the hearts and minds of International Olympic Committee (IOC) delegates in 1993, they beefed up their campaign.

A leaked Johnson letter telling an IOC delegate that the bid committee could no longer afford to send his daughter to Georgetown University in Washington, D.C., set off a firestorm. A bid committee was at the University of Utah Medical Center.

Salt Lake and all Utah citizens were embarrassed. If ever there was a population and a state with a squeaky-clean reputation, it was Utah. The sale of corporate sponsorships plummeted, and SLOC needed help. A search committee quickly singled out Mitt Romney as the white knight. Romney was a Massachusetts venture capitalist with a reputation for turning around failing companies and reselling them for big profits. If

Mass cross-country race start at Soldier Hollow in the Heber Valley. This Olympic legacy site is now open for public use.

paying college tuition for an IOC delegate's daughter? The stated IOC gift limit was $200!

The story didn't break until after Salt Lake had won the 2002 Games. But it broke early enough to launch investigations by media worldwide, the U.S. Justice Department, the Utah Attorney General's office, the IOC and the Salt Lake Olympic Organizing Committee (SLOC) itself. Welch and Johnson cleaned out their desks. Then former SLOC board chairman Frank Joklik, who replaced Welch as SLOC president, also resigned.

Salt Lake bidders had spent a million dollars winning the hearts and minds and presumably the votes of at least 10 IOC members. The gifts included personal loans from Welch, college tuition, paid shopping sprees and even orthopedic surgery for a visiting delegate

ever there was an organization in need of a turnaround artist, it was the Salt Lake Organizing Committee after the scandal broke. It helped that Romney was a Mormon, a graduate of Brigham Young University, and a vacation homeowner in the Park City area.

The IOC worked to salvage its own tarnished reputation, expelling six members and slapping the wrists of others. IOC President Juan Antonio Samaranch, not a humble man by any stretch of the imagination, had to face international television cameras and apologize to the people of Salt Lake City for the behavior of his members.

The bid scandal forced the IOC to rewrite its rules on bid-city campaigns, and it forced the SLOC to put on the best games possible (what it had wanted to do in the first place) in hopes of erasing all the negative publicity the city and state had endured.

Below: Head first, chin inches from ice, skeleton racers approach 90 miles an hour. Right: Mitt Romney, SLOC's turnaround artist. Below, right: Italian Bobsled Team push-starts at a World Cup race at Utah Olympic Park.

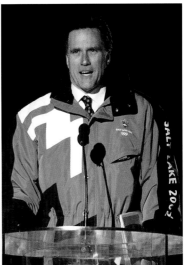

After the Romney turnaround, after the Games' closing ceremonies and the mass exodus of the Olympic traveling circus, Dick Ebersol, the president of NBC, which televised the Games, called them "far and away, the most successful Olympics, summer or winter, in history."

As for Romney, he left immediately for Boston to campaign for, and win, the governorship of Massachusetts.

Fortunately, the games left a second and more positive legacy—an infrastructure of Olympic competition venues second to none. The Utah Olympic Park near Kimball Junction outside of Park City; the Olympic Oval speed skating venue in Kearns, southwest of Salt Lake City; and the Soldier Hollow cross-country and biathlon venue in the Heber Valley, over the mountains in the next valley south of Park City, are all now well into their post-Olympic lives.

Now anyone with the money and the reservation can sit in the middle two seats of a four-man bobsled, often with a U.S. Bobsled Team driver and brakeman ahead and behind, and career down the track, pulling six g's in the turns. The ride is like a 45–second-long car wreck with all the twists and turns and bumps down the icy trough. Tourist riders often wake up the next morning feeling sore from muscles being stretched in the short, turbulent rocket shot downhill.

The Olympic Park does more than thrill tourists. It fulfills the goals of the USOC, to have first-class training facilities available for rising athletes. The park's nordic ski jumps are busy all winter with everything from training to World Cup competitions. The bobsled, luge and skeleton track does triple duty as three training venues, and between the two, the off-season splash pool and trampoline deck serve freestylers looking for summer air. Freestylers can ski down slippery ceramic-coated summer ramps, jump off kickers to practice their tricks and land in the huge

Utah Olympic Park operates year-round. The splash pool allows summer freestyle training. Summer jumping competitions attract network television coverage and big crowds.

splash pool injected with air bubbles to soften the water landings from 50 feet or more up. Winter freestyle hills allow year-round training on tricks practiced first on the poolside trampolines.

Olympic Park is also home to Utah's most unusual high school. Each summer, as the rest of the nation's school population goes on vacation, students of the Park City Winter School are deep into their studies. The accredited Winter School was created to allow serious student winter athletes to leave home for extended trips to winter competitions and still complete their studies. Now alpine racers, snowboarders, ski jumpers, freestylers and any winter athlete can go to school in their sport's off-season, while training after school in some of the world's finest facilities. The school also attracts other athletes, from golfers to equestrians, who want winters free for their competition schedules.

Park City Winter School is tucked behind the Joe Quinney Winter Sports Center and Alf Engen Ski Museum. The spectacular building stands next to the splash pool and displays the history of the Olympic Games in Utah, as well as tells the story of Utah skiing from its earliest days.

In the Heber Valley, the Soldier Hollow cross-country and biathlon venue is part of Wasatch Mountain State Park, a sprawling park with golf courses, fishing ponds, hiking and biking trails, and now one of the world's top cross-country skiing facilities open to athletes and the public, served with ample snowmaking through the winter.

In the Salt Lake Valley, the Olympic Oval completes the package of new athlete-training facilities open to the public. All three venues now are supported by an endowment consisting of Olympic profits from 2002.

If the Games served Utah well for 17 days, these legacy sites will serve a lifetime for aspiring local athletes and athletes worldwide who move here to train. The facilities, along with the U.S. Ski and Snowboard Team headquarters, are making Park City an attractive place to live for hundreds of athletes with their own Olympic dreams.

ABOVE: JANICA KOSTELIC OF CROATIA, WINNER OF THE WOMEN'S GS ON C.B.'S IN EAGLE ARENA. LEFT: GOLD MEDALIST KOSTELIC FLANKED BY SILVER MEDALIST ANJA PAERSON OF SWEDEN (LEFT), AND SONJA NEF, BRONZE MEDALIST FROM SWITZERLAND.

Some crew members even had time to take in some events as spectators. With PCMR's venue idle, Deer Valley's cranked up with freestyle aerials, with the silver taken by hometown Olympian Joe Pack.

While this was going on, Karen Korfanta took over as chief of race for the giant slalom at Eagle Race Arena. For Korfanta this was old hat. She'd worked every World Cup at Park City since the first one in 1985. If there was a weak spot on the C.B.'s GS course, it was up at the start. Years earlier the FIS had wanted a longer GS course, so the start was moved up Ski Team Ridge a little, on a slight grade any novice skier could handle with ease. For the Olympics, that flat start was beefed up with an incredible mound of snow 20 feet high and 30 feet wide.

a risk, but I think it made a difference."

The PCMR crews now had some time to breathe. It would be six days before their next and final competition, their bread-and-butter event, a men's giant slalom down C.B.'s on February 21, with the women's GS the next day.

BODE MILLER GOES FOR BROKE ON C.B.'S. HIS HEROIC SECOND GS RUN PULLED HIM FROM SEVENTH INTO SECOND. HIS SILVER MEDAL WAS AMERICA'S TENTH IN SKIING AND SNOWBOARDING.

ABOVE: STEPHAN EBERHARTER OF AUSTRIA CAPPED HIS CAREER WITH THE GOLD MEDAL IN THE GIANT SLALOM ON FEBRUARY 21, 2002. LEFT: BODE MILLER, USA, SILVER, STEPHAN EBERHARTER, AUSTRIA, GOLD, AND LASSE KJUSS, NORWAY, BRONZE, CELEBRATE AT EAGLE ARENA.

"It was huge," Korfanta marvels. "You stood up there, and you could look right [down] into the stadium. And if you were in the stadium, you could look up and see the start." In all previous World Cup races, the first glimpse spectators below had was when racers made an abrupt right off the flats and dropped straight onto Gotcha Face, the steepest section of the course and the one where the most crashes occur.

"If you don't set up right, you're probably going to miss a gate on this face and that's just how it is," Korfanta says with no apologies. From Gotcha Face the grade mellows out a bit as racers get to the grade road, a terrain feature courtesy of the Crescent tram, a century-old mining railroad that once chugged across the slope here. Then racers need to set up for C.B.'s face, another steep section leading toward the finish line.

"This course works well for both girls and guys. Both start in the same place. The best are going to win," Korfanta

SONJA NEF OF SWITZERLAND STREAKS TO HER BRONZE MEDAL GS FINISH ON C.B.'S, ON PARK CITY MOUNTAIN RESORT'S LAST DAY OF OLYMPIC COMPETITION.

explains on a tour of the course.

On Day 13 of the Games, with the Olympics winding down, a familiar GS field showed up on a familiar course. The weather held cold and clear. The course was hard. Conditions once again were perfect.

At the end of the first run, American hopes looked dim. Bode Miller, America's hottest male skier in years and already a silver medalist in these Games (in the combined downhill and slalom at Snowbasin a week earlier) stood in seventh. Stephan Eberharter, a stalwart of the always strong Austrian ski team, stood at the top of the leader board, hunting for his first gold medal in his last Olympics. Miller seemed out of the running.

But there are second chances in this sport. In his second run, Miller skied fast and reckless, on the ragged edge of control. "We held our breath," Bill Marolt says of the second run. "When he got down he was in first place, and then you got down to the last few guys."

Eberharter skied the course last. He let his skis run, didn't make any mistakes and bumped Miller into silver medal position by just 0.48 seconds over two runs. Miller's silver brought the U.S. Ski and Snowboard Team its 10th medal.

At the end of the day at Eagle Race Arena, Mark Menlove and Charlie Lansche broke open a bottle of scotch hidden at their Olympic press office. "C.B.'s picture was on the wall—a classic picture where he had a grin on his face like he had the world by its tail," Lansche says. "We poured a shot to C.B. and his memory, and you could just feel him in the room. It was very fitting." ⌁

MAREK SASIADEK OF POLAND GOING BIG IN THE EAGLE SUPERPIPE. SNOWBOARD LEGEND
JAKE BURTON TOLD SLOC OFFICIALS, "THIS WAS THE BEST SNOWBOARD COMPETITION ON
THE PLANET—EVER."

CHAPTER 8

A YEAR IN THE PARK

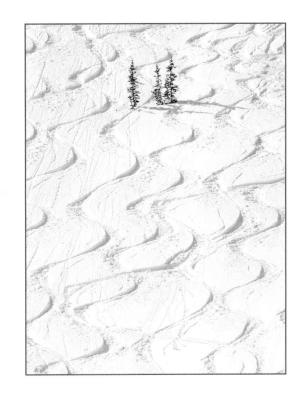

It was early morning. Conditions were perfect, with a clear blue sky and stillness in the air. The snow from storms and snow guns was packed and groomed to a depth of at least four feet. It was November 1994, about a week before the first World Cup race in the new Eagle Race Arena, on a newly cut run called C.B.'s.

A helicopter arrived. Nick Badami climbed into the left front seat as his wife, Avis, watched from the Eagle base area. Meanwhile, resort president Phil Jones, on skis, stood near the top of C.B.'s. It was still early enough that resort workers hadn't arrived to continue race preparations. The moment was perfect—and private.

The Jet Ranger slowly climbed up C.B.'s, moving back and forth across the run as it rose. Inside, Nick Badami opened an urn and, through his open window, began spooning his son's ashes over the run. Eagle Arena was finished now, and it was time to celebrate the moment of its arrival on the world ski scene. As the helicopter climbed, from C.B.'s face, to the Grade, and up Gotcha Face, Jones took pictures as tears

LEFT: ACROSS PARK MEADOWS GOLF COURSE TO THE MOUNTAIN. ABOVE:
FIRST TRACKS ON THE "GREATEST SNOW ON EARTH.™"

ABOVE: JUPITER PEAK. UNTIL CRAIG BADAMI
OPENED IT UP, IT WAS AVAILABLE ONLY TO
HEARTIEST BACKCOUNTRY SKIERS. RIGHT:
QUITTING TIME ON A SNOWY AFTERNOON.

rolled down his cheeks. The helicopter lifted higher and headed
up Ski Team Ridge, where Edgar Stern's crew had originally cut
training runs for the U.S. Ski Team, then on to Jupiter Peak and
the wide-open bowls that Craig Badami pushed to get opened to
the public. Nick Badami spread the rest of Craig's ashes there,
then returned to Eagle Race Arena to land.

While most people may measure a year beginning with the first
day of January, time is measured differently in a ski town. In Park
City, the year starts when you hear the first, distant *whoosh* of the
snowmaking guns starting up in the fall. On both sides of C.B.'s
run, snow gun after snow gun fires up, shooting white flakes onto
the brown grass. The emerging pattern of brown and white is like
a confirmation of other fall events already happening in the Park.

ABOVE, LEFT: FIRST UP GETS THE CORDUROY. ABOVE:
MAIN STREET, NOW ACCESSIBLE BY CHAIRLIFT. LEFT:
SNOWMAKING GOES ON ALL SEASON LONG.

The Gart Sports Sniagrab sale has come and gone. So, too, the huge Park City Ski Team Ski Swap at the high school, an unbelievable mass of people and gear in search of each other.

A year in the Park, as locals often refer to their town, is beginning.

Those first results of snowmaking inevitably melt away in the next warm spell, but eventually the snowmaking siege takes hold, and ribbons of white descend C.B.'s and its neighboring slalom run, Picabo's, named for Park City resident and the resort's one-time director of skiing Picabo Street.

Soon it's Thanksgiving and time for America's Opening, the official start of the World Cup racing season. Early skiers find good skiing on the machine-covered runs, and quite often the natural snow falls early. The resort has recorded opening days as early as late October, but World Cup weekend in late November is a more reliable start date.

Mostly it's locals who ski or snowboard in November. Then suddenly one Saturday before Christmas, as you wait in a long checkout line at the grocery store, it hits you: The tourists are back. The pace of resort town life picks up, and for those in the ski business, it's a wild, exhausting ride until the sun beats down

HOLLYWOOD, PARK CITY STYLE, AS THE SUNDANCE FILM FESTIVAL TAKES OVER TOWN FOR ITS JANUARY RUN.

in April and dictates an end to another season.

In between, a lot happens. The PIBs arrive in late January. These are the People In Black, who come from Hollywood—emotionally, if not physically. They come for the Sundance Film Festival, which was born in Robert Redford's head decades ago as a showcase for independent film. The event takes over the town, and it seems as if everyone on the street is dressed head to toe in black, looking cold and miserable every moment they're outside. To the outdoors-loving locals, the PIBs look pale and unhealthy. As happens at ski towns everywhere when urban nonskiers come to town, they become the butt of jokes.

But in recent years Sundance has become a vitally important arena for doing business and making a name for oneself in "the industry," as Hollywood calls itself. New stars are discovered here. Deals get done, sometimes on the chairlift. Fistfights have been known to break out in Park City restaurants as two studio execs duke it out over distribution rights. Parkites try to remain aloof

and not get impressed by the glitz. Film critic Roger Ebert parked illegally in front of a theater for a screening and got his car towed. Once the very visible star of a network sitcom, resplendent in a full-length fur coat, stood in line at Albertson's supermarket. When it came time for payment, the actor pulled out a checkbook and, since he was from out of state, was asked to produce two forms of ID for the checker. Behind him, the rest of the line cracked up. When word hits the street that Bruce Springsteen was dining in a basement restaurant, a steady parade of gawkers casually strolled through, hoping for a nod from the Boss. But a local get impressed? Never.

If a local has to decide between pursuing a J. Lo sighting or making tracks through fresh powder, the decision is not even close. But Sundance reminds the locals that their town, a broken-down old ghost in the '50s, is now solidly on the map. When *Entertainment Tonight* reporters simply say they're in Park City without the need to explain that they're talking about

ABOVE, LEFT: ACADEMY AWARD WINNER KEVIN SPACEY AUTOGRAPHS. ABOVE: PIBs STEVE BUSCEMI AND WILLEM DEFOE DEPART THE EGYPTIAN ON UPPER MAIN. LEFT: THE EGYPTIAN THEATER WITH A 1936 DOUBLE FEATURE.

Utah, the locals know they've arrived.

Parkites were not even impressed by the President of the United States. Two winters in a row, the Clintons stopped by for long ski weekends. Both times, President Clinton prowled Main Street while Hillary and Chelsea skied. At Dolly's Book Store, the leader of the free world picked out some books on China, which he was about to visit, but had his credit card rejected by the clerk. His American Express card had expired the month before, so Bill Clinton had to hit up his Secret Service agent to close the purchase.

The calendar flips to February and Presidents' Day weekend, which, along with Martin Luther King Day, generates Christmas-size crowds again. A lot of locals seem to believe that "March is the snowiest month," but the fact is that snow falls about equally in January, February and March. Equality is good. The Park City ski season spreads out about five months from first tracks to last.

When mud season arrives, many shops and restaurants close, and it seems the whole town leaves. They're all mountain biking

Snowboards Come to the Park

Since the first Norseman split some wood and fastened boards to his feet, skiers have put one ski on each foot and moved over the snow.

Jake Burton, Tom Sims and a handful of snowboarding pioneers changed all that in the late 1970s, and snowboarding took off in the '80s. Early snowboarders were young and exuberant. Too many of them

Park City welcomed snowboarders in 1996–1997 after a ban that snowboarders vilified. Its terrain parks today are among the best in the resort business.

behaved poorly, generating complaints from older, more conservative skiers. With skier-boarder collisions on the rise, a number of resorts reacted by banning snowboarding.

Park City Ski Area was one of them. "We felt it was something we didn't want to be involved with," former president and general manager Phil Jones says. "There was an awful lot of bad language being used. We saw ourselves as a high-end resort, and [snowboarders] represented the counterculture."

Deer Valley adopted the same policy, along with Alta. But Park City marketed itself as a family resort where every family member and ability level could find what he or she wanted. With kids taking up boarding in large numbers, Mom, Dad and the kids could no longer spend the day together because the kids would have to head over to nearby ParkWest ski area (now The Canyons) with their snowboards.

"Every year we'd talk about it," Jones remembers. Eventually,

snowboarders policed themselves and maturity brought respectability. Still, the Park City ban remained.

"I had to defend that policy every year," former resort public relations director Charlie Lansche says. "And every year it got harder and harder." Snowboard writers started trashing Park City—the resort and the town—for the dual bans at Deer Valley and Park City. They wrote that the town

was "hostile" to snowboarders. It was hard to argue the point.

In 1996, with a new owner and a blessing from board member Nick Badami, the parent POWDR Corp. decided to test the waters by opening sister resort Alpine Meadows to snowboarding as an experiment. When Nick told his grandson, Nicholas, that Park City would continue to hold off,

the 11-year-old told his grandfather, "Oh, grandpa, you're going to lose a lot of money!"

That night, Badami called new owner John Cumming at home and suggested that they might as well open up Park City as well. In short order, a snowboarding school was organized, and word went out that effective with the 1996–97 season, boarders could ride the entire mountain. Phil Jones organized a free snowboard lesson day to get Park City thinking in a new direction. Jones himself strapped on a board to understand what was coming.

The long-standing name and logo "Park City Ski Area" was no longer viable. Cumming came up with "Mountain Resort" as an all-inclusive name, and soon other "ski" areas started calling themselves mountain resorts as well. A new logo in the shape of an oval belt buckle was quickly designed in time for the start of the season, a trail passing a pine tree and bisecting the words "Park City Mountain Resort."

The change affected more than just policy. On the mountain, the resort plowed big money into a freeriding initiative, to not just allow riding

but to encourage it. Without any in-house expertise in the sport, it brought in top consultants to design halfpipes and terrain parks. Within a few years, riders were singling out PCMR as one of the top resorts in the country for their sport.

When the Olympics came to Eagle Race Arena, all the U.S. medals in snowboarding—two halfpipe golds, the men's halfpipe sweep and Chris Klug's bronze in GS—sealed Park City Mountain Resort's reputation as a new mecca for snowboarding.

Now families are skiing and riding together, and management hasn't really fielded any serious complaints. The rowdy counterculture riders who turned resort managers off in the '80s have grown up, gotten responsible and even started having kids of their own.

And another evolutionary turn is taking place. Where young males once headed to the top of the mountain to conquer Jupiter and assert their manhood, they now gravitate toward the bottom of the mountain, where the rails, table tops, boxes, pipes and all the rest give them a completely different challenge.

in southern Utah's red rock country. Those who avoid the Park City scene in Moab wind up at the mouth of Zion Canyon, in Springdale, Utah, bumping into neighbors on the hiking trails. Or they're visiting Mexico or Hawaii.

The trees leaf out late at 7,000 feet, but when they do, another Park City summer is underway. Payday lift reopens to haul mountain bikes for miles of single-track riding. Kayakers take day trips to the Provo River or the Weber. Fly-fishing enthusiasts find some legendary brown trout on the lower Provo. They've also got the Upper Provo and the Weber handy for the rainbows.

Boaters need just five minutes to exit town and end up on the Jordanelle Reservoir, one of the water supplies for the Wasatch Front. If Jordanelle is too busy, there's more open water within another 15 minutes at either Deer Creek, Echo or Rockport reservoirs. Other lake people—generally the Midwestern transplants—have established a Park City beachhead at Bear Lake, two hours north on the Idaho line.

Try to count Park City's golf courses. They sprout like mush-

rooms in Maine, usually surrounded by golf-in golf-out homes. Add endless hiking possibilities and a climate guaranteeing weeks of perpetual sunshine and cool evenings, and it's no wonder Park City is a thriving summer destination as well.

Summer brings a festival for every taste. Chamber music, bluegrass, jazz, rock and roll and symphony all have their weekends. When the first weekend in August arrives, Main Street becomes a pedestrian thoroughfare as thousands stroll up and down, shopping for artistic works at the Park City Arts Festival.

You'll hear it said often around town: "I came for the winter,

ASPEN TREES DOMINATE THE FORESTS AROUND PARK CITY. IT'S TIME FOR ONE LAST HIKE OR RIDE THROUGH AUTUMN GLORY BEFORE WINTER SETS IN.

ABOVE: GOLF COURSES DESIGNED BY GOLF'S GREATEST PLAYERS AND ARCHITECTS ARE TURNING PARK CITY INTO A SUMMER GOLFING DESTINATION. RIGHT: THE PARK CITY ARTS FESTIVAL DRAWS TENS OF THOUSANDS OF ART LOVERS TO MAIN STREET EACH AUGUST.

but I stayed for the summers."

Spring and summer also bring the rat-a-tat-tat of nail guns, as predictable a sound as November's snow guns. Park City and growth have had a four-decade love-hate relationship.

Growth here is hard to disguise. This is not Vermont or Montana, where trees dominate the natural landscape and a whole housing project can be hidden behind a curtain of ever-greens or hardwood trees. Park City lies at the edge of the Great Basin Desert. In a good year 350 inches of snow may fall in Jupiter, but the basin below at 7,000 gets far less. The result is a natural landscape dominated by the lowly sagebrush. When a building goes up here, it's noticed.

It was hard to miss when K mart broke ground at Kimball Junction for a Big K store. One morning, protestor Todd Gabler chained himself to a backhoe that was ready to begin the excavation. Sheriff Fred Eley showed up personally to get out bolt cutters to slice through the chain, but not before TV cameras captured the scene. Gabler's point got wide attention.

The controversy had its roots in the fact that two different governmental bodies guide the future of the Park City area. The city limits extend from the ground south of White Pine Canyon

MINERS USED TO CURSE THE APPROACH OF WINTER. NOW WINTER IS THE WELCOME START OF THE SKI SEASON. THE TOWN LIFT (IN CENTER) BROUGHT SKIING TO MAIN STREET.

Road, where the new St. Mary's Catholic Church sits, to the ridgetops of Park City and Deer Valley resorts and east to Highway 40. Outside city limits, Summit County controls zoning and growth. The three-member Summit County Commission in the past was represented by two east-county members and one from Park City. Until recently, the more conservative east-county members didn't care much for telling people what they could do—or not do—with their property. Kimball Junction is the result, a sprawl of mismatched commercial districts with confusing and even dangerous traffic patterns. The K mart started a flood of development there. Its construction so enraged locals that many refused to shop there. They went across Highway 224 to Wal-Mart, which is set back on a hillside above the highway and nearly invisible until you reach it. When K mart got into financial trouble nationwide, the nearly empty Kimball Junction store was among the first closed.

To prevent urban sprawl from creeping closer, Park City's town government got out its checkbook. In a deal that stunned nearly everyone who read about it in *The Park Record*, the city wrote a check for the Osguthorpe Farm, a parcel of land reaching from White Pine Canyon to the Aspen Springs development past the dairy barn heading into town. The large white barn, originally the McPolin family dairy barn, now sits at Park City's entrance in a sea of grass—open space that will remain so forever.

Park City did not stop there. Twice voters have approved tax increases to pay for bonds to buy more open space. The city's goal is to surround itself with a greenbelt "moat" to keep the city separate and distinct from the Snyderville Basin, now teeming with subdivisions and commercial development.

Summit County is now seeing the light too, employing inno-

THE TOWN OF PARK CITY BOUGHT THE OSGUTHORPE FARM WITH THE MCPOLIN DAIRY BARN TO PRESERVE THE OPEN SPACE ALONG PARK CITY'S ENTRY CORRIDOR. THIS VIEW LOOKS NORTH, TOWARD THE CANYONS RESORT.

ABOVE: PARK CITY IN ITS AUTUMN GLORY. SOON THE FIRST SNOW WILL OUTLINE THE RUNS WITH RIBBONS OF WHITE. RIGHT: PARK CITY'S HISTORIC OLD TOWN CHARMS VISITORS AND LOCALS ALIKE.

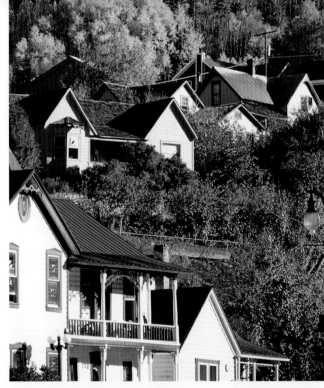

vative land preservation techniques to protect open space and channel development to where it is more appropriate. The best example is at The Canyons. When the American Skiing Co. bought the old Park West ski area, which had been renamed Wolf Mountain under a different ownership group, it wanted to develop a high-density base village of hotel and condominium buildings to provide beds to feed into its lifts.

The Canyons, private landowners and Summit County agreed to do some horse trading. A landowner with approved density rights out in the dwindling open space of the Snyderville Basin was allowed to transfer those development rights for development rights of equal value at The Canyons. With a new property right at The Canyons, the "sending" property lost its development rights and became open space. The transfer of development rights (TDR) concept has now preserved large land holdings in the basin from development. Much of that land has become part of the Swaner Nature Preserve, run by a private nonprofit group dedicated to preserving and restoring the basin ecosystem of the lands between Kimball Junction and the subdivisions that surround it.

Smarter growth is the wave of the future, and with Park City

surrounding itself with its sagebrush moat, the chances of urban sprawl stealing the charm of the place is diminished.

Nick Badami is a man who speaks in short, blunt sentences. In 1993, he sold an 80 percent share of his ski holding company, Alpine Meadows of Tahoe, Inc., to the Cumming family of Salt

184

GETTING AIR THE OLD FASHIONED WAY. LEFT: JOHN CUMMING OF POWDR CORPORATION PLANS TO KEEP THE FOCUS ON THE MOUNTAIN.

found it in the family of Ian Cumming, the head of a New York City-based investment company.

Cumming's oldest son, John, was interested in the outdoor business. He'd been working as a climbing guide and founder of an outdoor clothing line, Mountain Hardwear. John was looking for his niche, and like Craig Badami before him, it wasn't a buttoned-down life in corporate America. The two families started talking.

"I liked the family, liked their reputation. It was a good combination," Badami explains. "I was looking for someone who would treat my employees the way we had in the past—not some conglomerate."

John Cumming set out to learn the business at Nick's side. He learned the business end of a paintbrush and shovel, worked as a reservationist in a cubicle and got to know each department. Badami shared his office with him. "To Nick's credit, he came to work every day and sat back and watched me do things, some of them really dumb in the beginning and some not so dumb, and he handled it all with incredible grace," says Cumming.

Lake City, explaining, "I was getting older and my son was dead."

Badami had been approached many times through the years by big ski corporations with a number of resort properties. He was not interested in selling his family's business to an impersonal corporation. He'd been looking for the right ownership group and

Loran Larsen Park

In the earliest years of Treasure Mountains Resort, underground hard-rock miners suddenly found themselves aboveground, working ski resort jobs. One of those who traded his hard hat for a ski hat was Loran Larsen. Today, the Park City trail map honors him with the name "Loran Larsen Park" at the top of Assessment, an intermediate cruiser accessible from the Bonanza and Silverlode chairs.

"Loran took pride in everything he did," recalls former longtime the Greater Park City Corp. years. One day they were test-driving a new groomer, with Larsen driving. "There must have been about three feet of snow," he says. "We were at the top of Silver Skis and immediately got going too fast. It's a good thing it was bowl shaped or we'd have been in the trees. We about had to upchuck when we got out!"

"[Woody] never jumped in a snowcat with my dad again!" Larsen's son Les Larsen remembers.

Loran Larsen at the employee-declared "State Park." Twenty years of hard-rock mining led to 30 more aboveground as the indispensable heavy equipment operator and snow groomer for the resort.

area manager Phil Jones. "He was the kind of guy who did things his way—the mining way—but he'd always get it done."

Larsen was the resort's jack-of-all-trades. He knew where every water, sewer and power line was buried without consulting a map. There are lots of stories about "Longbelly Larsen."

"He had a pretty good-sized belly, and his relatives would call him Uncle Longbelly, so we called him Longbelly, too" Jones says. "I don't know why he survived [the transition from mining to skiing when others didn't] but he ended up in the right department with equipment, trail work and snow grooming."

Larsen cut many of the original ski runs for United Park City Mines. Then, as the resort took off, he gravitated toward grooming them. "He was a nifty guy," remembers Woody Anderson, the general manager of

"He'd come in every year and say, 'I gotta have a few days off, my pipes are frozen, I've gotta unthaw my pipes'—it was always '*unthaw* my pipes,'" Jones remembers. Larsen wasn't a talker, and much of what he did say was unprintable. He didn't warm up to other employees all that well.

"He was very quiet—salty [and] abrasive—until he accepted you," Les Larsen says. "It was epic when he'd say, 'How are you doing?'"

One winter when the sewer lines froze at the Summit House Restaurant, Jones ordered 18 portable toilets to the Summit to keep it operating. Every night they froze, and every night Jones had to round up whomever he could find to trek to the top and chip out the frozen you-know-what. "Some guys I had to give a fifth of whiskey [to do that job], but Loran was one of those guys who would be there just to help.

He was a guy you could count on."

With his mastery of heavy equipment, Larsen gravitated to snow grooming. For years he was in charge of the grooming fleet. He and Jones hand-made rollers and other grooming attachments in the years before they were commercially available.

Larsen parked his grooming equipment in a big flat area to the right of the top of Assessment. Longtime resort maintenance employee and writer Jay Meehan would organize a ski group every year for his buddies from Heber City, 17 miles away, where Meehan lives. Meehan called it "HeberSki." Larsen would always arrive early for HeberSki and groom the snow to perfection for the group's annual picnic, held near the same area where Larsen parked his grooming machines. Meehan's mainte-nance department was in charge of painting trail signs, so he had one made that said LORAN LARSEN STATE PARK and posted at the spot.

Longbelly Larsen retired in 1996, and Les Larsen took over as head of the grooming department. Within six months, Longbelly was bored and back working for his son. Cancer slowed him down, but he licked it temporarily. When he died at age 70 in July 1998, his family spread his ashes at Loran Larsen State Park (now marked on the resort's trail map as Loran Larsen Park).

His friends still gather each August at Clyde's Billiards in Heber to celebrate his birthday. Jay Meehan started the "Longbelly Log Book" so the celebrants could record their thoughts on the big day. Among the entries so far: "To our groomin' mate, smooth'n the clouds in 308." Also: "We remain a ship adrift, in need of your ornery-ass rud-der." Les Larsen wrote, "You would have loved this! Bullshit flying, Copenhagen bein' spit, [and] stories, stories, stories!"

No one adapted better than Loran Larsen to his changing town. Twenty years underground as a hard-rock miner led to 30 years above-ground as the indispensable person who kept the ski area running.

"Everybody in the company loved the man," Meehan says. "Everybody."

IN 1964, JIM MCCONKEY HIKED UP WHAT WOULD BE CALLED MCCONKEY'S BOWL AND TUCKED ALL THE WAY DOWN. MORE RECENTLY, PETER WEISS CAUGHT MCCONKEY'S CHAIR AND MADE SOME SINUOUS TRACKS.

Park City Mountain Resort today is the flagship of POWDR Corp., now the Cumming's ski property holding company, which also owns the original Badami acquisition, Alpine Meadows, as well as Boreal Ridge on Donner Pass in the Sierra Nevada and Mt. Bachelor near Bend, Oregon.

Badami is now a minority shareholder in the company he built. He remains on the board of directors, and he and John Cumming talk frequently. "Nick is a giant. He's provided a huge amount of leadership, and my family would do anything for him," John says.

Under the new ownership, a flurry of changes and spending began spinning heads again. From the 1993 acquisition to the start of the 21st century, the new owners have installed more high-speed six-pack lifts than any other resort in the world: Payday, Bonanza, Silverlode and McConkey's.

With the Payday-Bonanza combination, six times more skiers can reach the Summit House in 10 fewer minutes. With the new lifts in place, the venerable gondola came down, a victim of the need for speed in getting to the top. With installation of the Town Bridge in 2001, skiers coming down Creole or Quittin' Time can now ski right onto Main Street's new, lower sections. Much of lower Main, built with various facades and setbacks, actually disguises the mass of a new Marriott condominium hotel.

With snowboards allowed on the mountain, the resort aggressively courted the new clientele with a dizzying number of terrain parks and features, like the 2001 cutting of Heckler run off Payday, where a new terrain park is a focus of young riders. A new superpipe on Payday complements the Eagle Pipe, the competition halfpipe which is off-limits to recreational riders.

The resort also revived and updated a simple form of fun Otto Carpenter hosted at his Snow Park a half century earlier. In 1999 it bought a defunct beginners ski area near Parley's Summit and turned it into a night lighted tubing park where riders can scream downhill through steep troughs of snow divided into various tubing lanes. The new snow play area is called Gorgoza Tubing Park.

ABOVE AND LEFT: FRESHIES FOR ALL.

mountain at the Payday base area. With a new hotel on Main served by the Town lift, and the one next to Payday lift, the resort, working with developers, has beefed up the number of "hot beds" available for nightly rental to destination skiers.

To improve skier services, the original 1963 heart of the resort—the gondola base lodge—was torn down in 1999 and replaced with the Legacy Lodge, a combination restaurant, tavern, locker room and shopping center built, like the Marriott next door, in the style and look of an old mining building.

John's brother David, a chef by training and a partner with his brother in Mountain Hardwear, has joined POWDR Corp., concentrating on improvements in guest services, including major upgrades in food quality. The remodeled, upgraded look of the Summit House is one example.

The changes are substantial, and the resort is constantly evolving. Although the resort has reentered one side business—retail ski and board rentals—the Cummings aren't interested in getting spread too thin. The resort's most valuable property is its parking lots, and a master plan is approved and in place to build hotels, condominiums and a mix of other facilities on the lots and move the skier parking underground. The resort will not sell the land for less than the cost of constructing replacement parking, and so far no developer has stepped in with the kind of money necessary to

For years, many of Park City's condominiums have been turned into permanent homes for year-round residents. Others are simply purchased and held out of the rental pool. Faced with a declining skier bed base, the resort negotiated to have the big Marriott Mountainside interval-ownership hotel located on

SHANNON NOBIS GREW UP IN PARK CITY, MADE THE U.S. SKI TEAM, RACED IN THE OLYMPICS, AND RARELY SLOWS DOWN.

OUT-OF-THIS-WORLD SKIING IN PARK CITY'S JUPITER BOWL.

accomplish that goal. Like their mentor, the Cumming family wants to focus on the business of running a ski and snowboard area. "We will never be a developer," John Cumming promises. "It's the snow," he says. "That's what matters."

The community's shift to skiing began in 1963 as a way to save the town by subsidizing the mine operations through the lean years. Forty years later, the final shoe dropped forever on mining. In 2003, Capital Growth Partners, a real estate investment firm, bought all the remaining assets of United Park City Mines. UPCM hadn't mined an ounce of ore in 21 years. Instead, it worked to secure city approvals to build on the last great expanse of undeveloped land in Park City. Flagstaff Bowl, the land between the boundaries of Park City Mountain Resort and Deer Valley, represents one of the last great opportunities for large-scale real estate development contiguous to an American ski resort. The place where Connor's soldiers found the first ore that set off the stampede for silver that created Park City is evolving

into its own enclave, situated between two resorts rated among the top 10 in America. With approvals in place for hotels, private homes, condominiums and ski runs, Flagstaff may be the next big thing in American skiing.

By mid August, clouds blow up over the Wasatch nearly every afternoon and rumble with thunder. Lightning starts streaking across the sky, and a short, welcome rain shower comes down and makes everything smell clean. It's a clear signal that the weather is unsettled, and changing.

By mid September the scrub oak starts turning red. Then one patch of aspen on the hill partway up Thaynes leads the change to gold. Soon the whole mountain quakes with golden aspen. After a peak week of stunning visuals, a big wind will invariably come along and clear the leaves off the aspens. The nights grow colder, and the progression continues:

Sniagrab. Ski swap. The *whoosh* of snow guns on the mountain. Another year in the Park is about to begin. ⌖

ACKNOWLEDGMENTS

The story of Park City is a big one. Writing it required a lot of help. To the following people I owe deep and heartfelt thanks:

To Vern Greco and Julie Hopkins at Park City Mountain Resort, plus longtime employees and storytellers Jay Meehan, Billy Gray, Brian Strait, Karen Korfanta, Molly Laramie, Jennie Smith and the last original employee—Clark Parkinson. Thanks also to John and David Cumming from POWDR Corporation.

To these longtime skiers, friends whose stories of town life I found both touching and funny:

Woody Anderson
Keith and Carol Bates
Bob Birkbeck (deceased)
David Chaplin
Marianne Cone
Judy Dykman
Alf Engen (deceased)
Stein Eriksen
Lloyd Evans
Peggy Fletcher
J.W. "Jack" Gallivan
Larry and Dixie Hethke
Tom Kelly
Gary Kimball
Mike Korologos
Charlie Lansche
Wilma and Ted Larremore
Les Larsen
Brigham Madson
Bill Marolt
Mark Menlove
Sandra Morrison
Phil Notarianni
Ross Powers
Harry Reed
Jim and Carol Santy
Harald Schoenhaar
Ella Sorenson
Edgar Stern
Hank Tauber
Bob Wright

Special thanks to Hal Compton, who guided me on skis around the mine ruins and through the files of the Park City Museum. To Phil Jones, who was at PCMR through nearly its entire existence and who did practically every job here from watering the golf course to serving as resort president. To Nick Badami, whose vision created the modern resort. To Mel Fletcher, a living history of Park City skiing. And to the Ol' Miner, Rich Martinez, the last man in Park City to earn his living as a hard rock miner.

Finally, this book would never have been completed without the confidence and skill of the team at Mountain Sports Press: Bill Grout, Michelle Schrantz, Scott Kronberg, Chris Salt and Paul Prince.

THANK YOU ONE AND ALL.

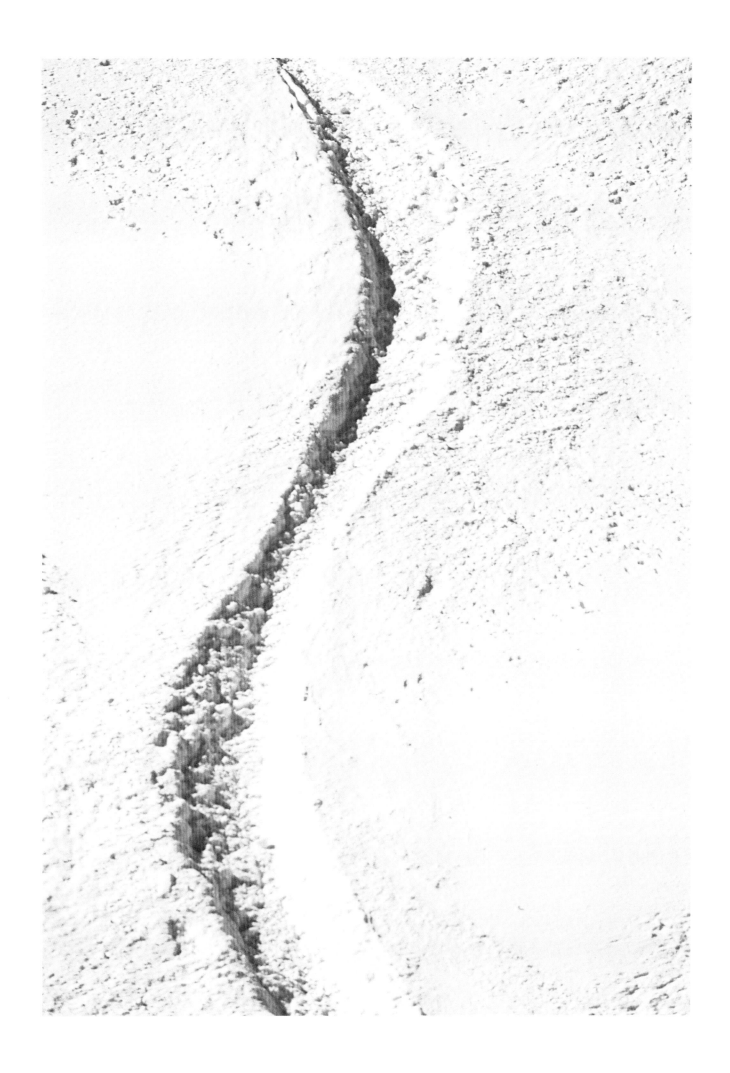

BIBLIOGRAPHY

Diggings and Doings in Park City
Raye Ringholz, 1972

Official Report of the XIX Olympic Games
SLOC, 2002

Skiing in Utah: A History
Alexis Kelner, 1980

Treasure Mountain Home
George A. Thompson and Fraser Buck, 1981

2002 Salt Lake City
The *Deseret News* Staff, 2002

Material also came from back issues of *Park City* magazine and its many talented writers.

PHOTO CREDITS

INDEX